This book belongs to:

....

DK LONDON

Edited by Clare Lloyd, James Mitchem
US Editor Jane Perlmutter
US Senior Editor Shannon Beatty
Project Art Editor Charlotte Bull
Text by Ben Hubbard, Wil Mara, Andrea Mills,
Joe Norbury, Becky Walsh, Graeme Williams
Designed by Hannah Moore, Rhys Thomas, Sadie Thomas
Managing Editor Penny Smith
Managing Art Editor Mabel Chan
Production Editor Dragana Puvavic
Production Controller John Casey
Jacket Designer Charlotte Bull
Jacket Co-ordinator Issy Walsh
Publishing Director Sarah Larter

DK DELHI

Senior Art Editor Nidhi Mehra
Assistant Editor Niharika Prabhakar
Project Picture Researcher Sakshi Saluja
Managing Editor Monica Saigal
Managing Art Editor Romi Chakraborty
Delhi Team Head Malavika Talukder

First American Edition, 2020
Published in the United States by DK Publishing
1450 Broadway, Suite 801, New York, New York 10018

A catalog record for this book is available from the Library of Congress.
ISBN: 978-1-4654-9974-5

DK books are available at special discounts when purchased in bulk
for sales promotions, premiums, fund-raising, or educational use.
For details, contact: DK Publishing Special Markets,
1450 Broadway, Suite 801, New York, New York 10018
SpecialSales@dk.com

Printed and bound in China

For the curious
www.dk.com

New Material Only
PA Reg No. 14954 (CN)
Content Polyurethane Foam

Matériaux neufs seulement	New Material Only
No. de permis: 1790-123	Reg No. 1790-123
Contenu: Mousse de polyuréthane	Content Polyurethane Foam

My Encyclopedia of
Very
IMPORTANT
ADVENTURES

DK

Contents

Scientists and inventors

Trailblazers and pioneers

Explorers and

discoverers

Throughout history, bold and daring people have **risked everything** to discover faraway lands and explore unfamiliar places. It takes a brave person to venture into the unknown, so take a deep breath, turn the page, and prepare for your very own adventure.

A trailblazing **translator**

This monk was a **super scholar** and traveler who helped introduce the religion of Buddhism to China.

Bold beginning

At the beginning of the 7th century, **Xuanzang** learned about Buddhism while studying sacred writings. He devoted his time to **translating** these ancient documents and soon converted to Buddhism. Xuanzang wanted to learn more about the religion, but the Chinese emperor had forbidden travel outside China.

Secret escape

One night, Xuanzang set off on a secret **pilgrimage to India**. He headed west, through deserts and mountains, meeting people from different cultures and faiths. In India, he sailed along the Ganges River, marveled at Buddhist sites, and studied alongside great thinkers.

Xuanzang wrote a book about his journey, filled with stories of the places he visited.

During his pilgrimage, Xuanzang traveled the Silk Road—a famous trade route.

King Harsha of North India thanked Xuanzang for his important work.

The pilgrim returns

16 years later, Xuanzang returned to China with a lot of new knowledge. The Chinese emperor delighted in hearing what Xuanzang had learned during his **adventures abroad**. As a result of his brave pilgrimage, the Buddhist faith spread to China and beyond.

Icelandic sagas contain a mix of fact and fiction, so we don't know the exact details of Leif's story.

Welcome to the land of grapes!

Viking voyage

Many people think Christopher Columbus was the first European to reach the **New World**, but it's likely he was beaten by about 500 years by this Viking sailor.

Like father, like son

According to ancient stories, or "sagas," the young Viking, **Leif Erikson**, grew up in Iceland. At the time, Vikings explored the seas and raided the lands for treasures. As the second son of legendary leader Erik the Red, who discovered Greenland, Erikson wanted to travel even farther than his father.

New World

Around 1000 CE, Erikson and his crew boarded a ship and set sail to find new lands. After passing Greenland, they continued west and found the **New World**. They landed on the east coast of what is now North America, at what is thought to be Newfoundland, Canada.

North America

Iceland

Erikson's route

L'Anse aux Meadows, the only known Viking settlement in North America, is thought to be Vinland, but archaeologists still aren't totally sure!

Erikson named the place "Vinland" because he found a lot of grapes growing there. After a few months, he sailed home, never to return again.

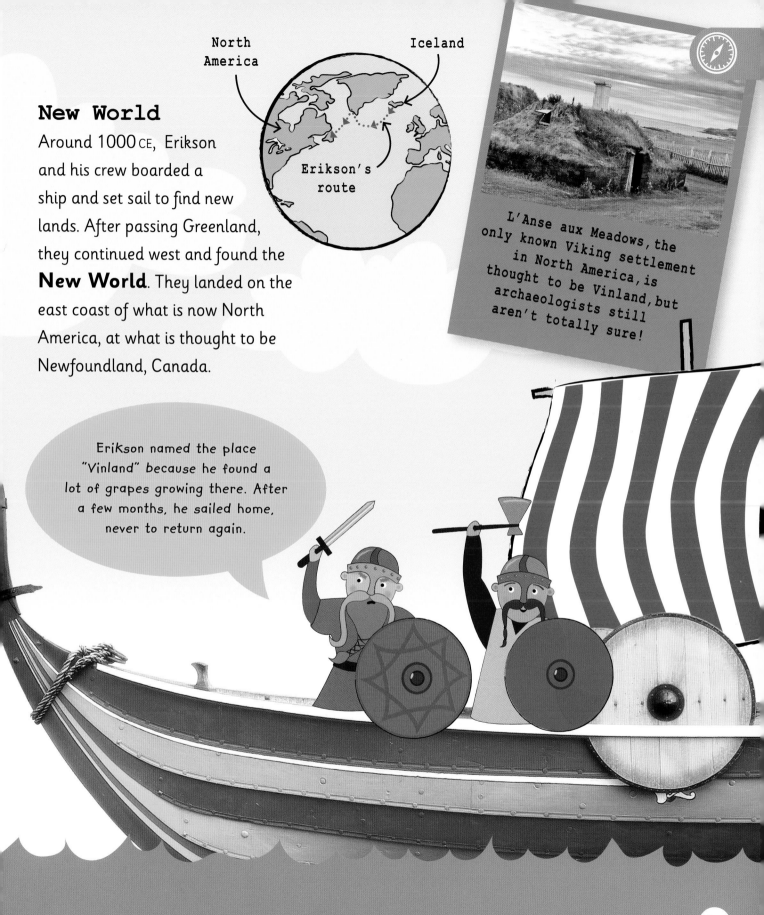

Exploring the **East**

When he was 17 years old, Italian merchant Marco Polo set off on a **journey to China**—and that was just the start of a series of unbelievable adventures.

Marco traveled with his father and uncle.

Europe

Venice

Eastern expedition

In 1271, the three Polos left Venice, Italy, and headed east. The Chinese emperor, **Kublai Khan**, had requested holy oil and a letter from the pope. For four years, they trekked along what is now known as the Silk Road, an ancient trading route, before arriving at the gates of Kublai Khan's magnificent palace in Shangdu, China.

Royal approval

Kublai Khan was delighted to see the three men and made Marco an important member of his royal court. For the next 17 years, Marco went on many trips through **Asia** on the emperor's behalf.

Asia

Marco's journey

Shangdu

Marco's return journey

Seeing is believing

Not many Europeans had ever traveled this far, and Marco was **amazed by what he saw**. He came across beautiful silks, tasty spices, and even kites and fireworks. But for Marco, most impressive of all was China's use of paper money instead of silver and gold.

East meets West

After Marco arrived home in 1295, he composed a book about his adventures. But people thought his stories were **hard to believe** and branded his book *Il Milione*, or "The Million Lies." To this day, nobody knows for sure how much of what he wrote is fact, and how much is fiction.

The Million Lies

The epic explorer

Bitten by the travel bug at a young age, this scholar spent 30 years exploring before writing about his adventures in one of the world's first **travel books**.

Holy pilgrimage

In 1325, Moroccan explorer **Ibn Battuta** turned 21 and set off on a religious pilgrimage to Mecca, in what is now Saudi Arabia. His trip was challenging, and he faced struggles with thieves and illness. He kept on going, however, and 16 months later he finally reached Mecca.

Today, millions of Muslims make a religious pilgrimage to Mecca each year.

Ibn Battuta

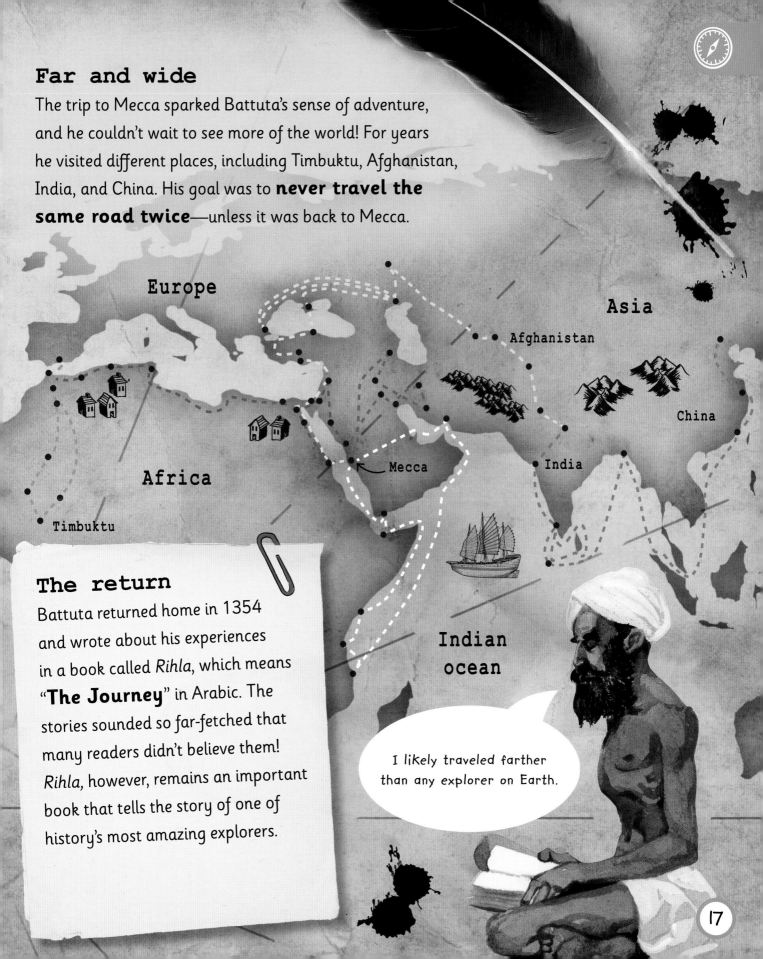

Far and wide

The trip to Mecca sparked Battuta's sense of adventure, and he couldn't wait to see more of the world! For years he visited different places, including Timbuktu, Afghanistan, India, and China. His goal was to **never travel the same road twice**—unless it was back to Mecca.

Europe

Asia

Afghanistan

China

Africa

Mecca

India

Timbuktu

The return

Battuta returned home in 1354 and wrote about his experiences in a book called *Rihla*, which means "**The Journey**" in Arabic. The stories sounded so far-fetched that many readers didn't believe them! *Rihla*, however, remains an important book that tells the story of one of history's most amazing explorers.

Indian ocean

I likely traveled farther than any explorer on Earth.

The treasure voyages

Between 1405 and 1433, **Zheng He** led the Chinese emperor's vast fleet of ships on seven great voyages.

The magnetic compass, invented in China, was probably used by Zheng to navigate the seas.

Glorious gifts

When he first set sail, Zheng was commander of a staggering 300 ships! The ships were filled with **gifts** such as silks and patterned plates, as well as hundreds of soldiers, astronomers, doctors, and scholars to impress the people he met on his voyages.

Man on a mission

Zheng's plan was to travel around Asia and Africa and spread the word about the Chinese emperor, **Yongle**. Even though he was already leader of a powerful empire, Yongle wanted to be world famous.

Emperor Yongle

Zheng returned with countless treasures and exotic animals.

Epic adventures

Zheng visited over 30 countries. He made many lands aware of China's power and returned with gifts, such as **ivory**, **spices**, and even a captured enemy king! His voyages were full of excitement—he stopped a pirate rebellion, and watched the crowning of an Indian king.

Naming the **Americas**

Have you ever wondered how North and South America got their names? Or who decided what they should be called?

Well bad news—it's still not very clear!

Amerigo Vespucci

During my time, people thought the world only had three parts: Europe, Africa, and Asia. That's why the Americas became known as the "New World."

The New World

The Italian explorer **Amerigo Vespucci** claimed to have discovered the "New World," on a voyage to what is now Brazil, in 1497. This isn't true though—both Christopher Columbus and the Viking Leif Erikson had sailed there before him, and native people had been living there for generations.

North America

Today, North America and South America are two separate continents.

Mapping the world

Although Amerigo wasn't the first to discover the New World, he made early voyages to it, and it is widely thought that he was the first European to realize it was a **separate continent.**

South America

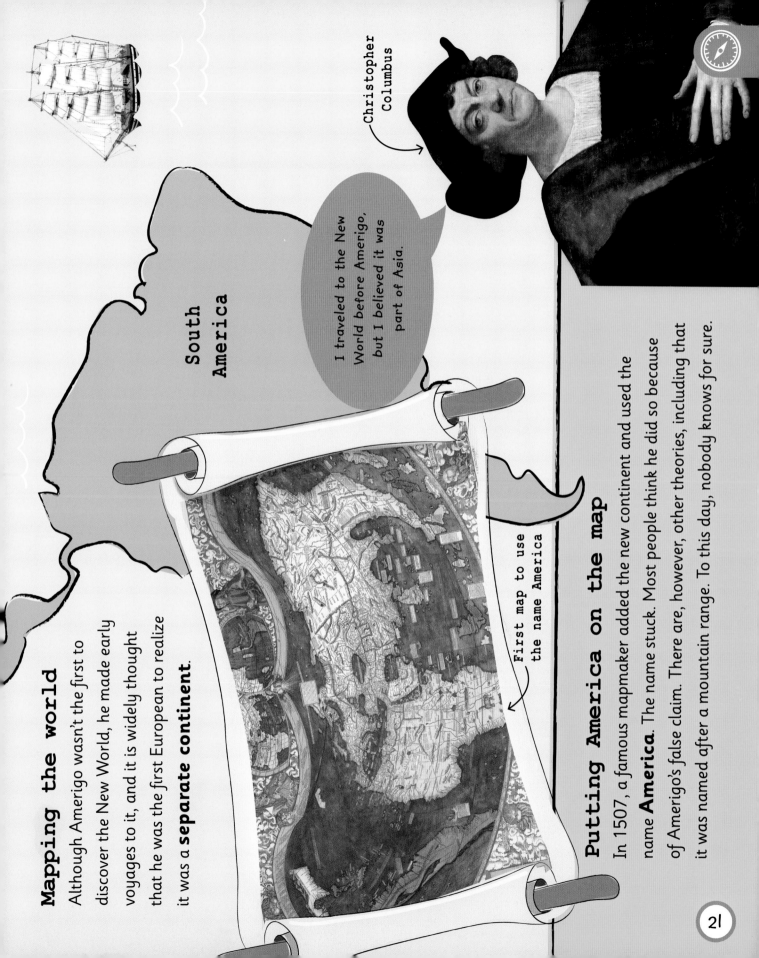

I traveled to the New World before Amerigo, but I believed it was part of Asia.

Christopher Columbus

First map to use the name America

Putting America on the map

In 1507, a famous mapmaker added the new continent and used the name **America.** The name stuck. Most people think he did so because of Amerigo's false claim. There are, however, other theories, including that it was named after a mountain range. To this day, nobody knows for sure.

Sailing around **the world**

In 1519, five ships, carrying more than 200 sailors, set off from Spain on a history-making voyage. Only 18 sailors made it back, becoming the first people to sail all the way **around the world**. Although that wasn't really the plan…

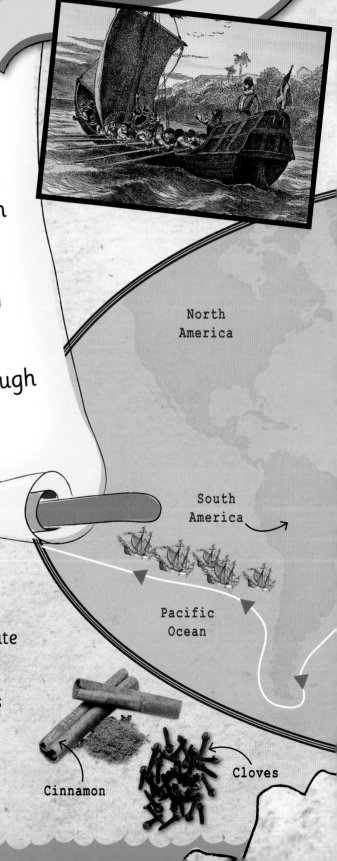

North America

South America

Pacific Ocean

Cash for cloves

King Charles I of Spain wanted to find a route for his ships to reach the **Spice Islands** (Maluku Islands in Indonesia). These islands were full of spices such as cloves, nutmeg, and cinnamon, which were very valuable.

Cinnamon

Cloves

Magellan's plan

A Portuguese sailor, **Ferdinand Magellan**, came up with a plan to sail **west** around the Americas to reach the Spice Islands. When the King of Spain approved, Magellan set off in 1519 with **five ships**.

Traveling all the way around something is called "circumnavigating."

Ferdinand Magellan

Fateful voyage

The journey was very **dangerous**, and the crew suffered storms, rebellion, disease, and starvation. After two years, only two ships made it to the Spice Islands, and Magellan himself was killed in battle on the way.

1519
Five ships leave Spain

Europe

Spain | START

1522
One ship makes it back

Africa

Asia

1521
Two ships arrive at the Spice Islands

SPICE ISLANDS

1521
Magellan is killed in battle in the Philippines

Indian Ocean

Australia

Pacific Ocean

Atlantic Ocean

Just one ship was seaworthy enough to make the return journey back to Spain.

Magellan and his sailors were among the first Europeans to see penguins.

A **golden** opportunity

This swashbuckling seaman sailed **around the world** for queen and country aboard the magnificent *Golden Hind*.

"It isn't that life ashore is distasteful to me. But life at sea is better."
—Francis Drake

Professional pirate Francis Drake grew up by the coast in England and became a **privateer** (officially approved pirate) in charge of seizing treasures from Spanish ships. Impressed by his plundering, Queen Elizabeth I asked Drake to head for South America to claim new lands.

The Spanish named Francis Drake

The Golden Hind was originally named Pelican.

Making waves

In 1577, Drake set sail aboard the *Golden Hind* with a small fleet of ships. He battled raging storms and Spanish ships. When he returned in 1580, not only did he bring back lots riches, but he had become the second person to captain a ship all the way **around the world**.

Golden Hind

A life at sea

A hero to some, but a villain to others, Drake was knighted for his efforts, becoming known as **Sir Francis Drake**. His daring adventures at sea continued when he played an important part in defeating the Spanish Armada, a fleet of 130 ships destined to invade England.

"EL DRAQUE," meaning "THE DRAGON."

The father of Chinese **travel**

Encouraged to travel by his mother, **Xu Xiake** spent about 30 years exploring his home country of China and writing about what he saw along the way.

On the move

At the time of Xu's travels in the early 1600s, China was ruled by the prosperous **Ming dynasty**. Xu was determined to see as much of his homeland as he could. He spent years having adventures such as eating dinner with a local ruler and sharing yak tongue, losing his shoes while crossing a dangerous river, and jumping overboard to escape pirates!

Battling bandits

Although Xu enjoyed his adventures, he faced plenty of **difficulties**. He was often robbed by bandits, forcing him to beg for food or rely on the kindness of strangers. On one occasion he read poetry in exchange for **mushrooms**!

Love of the outdoors

Xu loved **nature**. He once sat and listened to snow falling for a whole day and loved following rivers to find their sources. He ventured where few travelers had gone, including to a grotto, that legend said was home to a **dragon**!

The Travelogue of Xu Xiake

We know about Xu's travels because he wrote in a diary **every single day**. His writing helped map China and record the histories of previously unknown places. His diaries were eventually collected and published as *The Travelogue of Xu Xiake*.

Today, China's National Tourism Day is celebrated on May 19th, the date Xu first set off on his travels.

A great **pilgrimage**

Forbidden to practice their religious beliefs in England, a group of people called Pilgrims needed a fresh start. In 1620, they boarded a ship in search of a **new life**.

A perilous journey

In November 1620, after spending 66 days sailing across the Atlantic Ocean, the Pilgrims arrived at Massachusetts Bay, in what is now North America. They had battled harsh storms and difficult conditions, but their troubles weren't over. They struggled through the freezing cold weather without much **food or shelter**.

THANKSGIVING is now celebrated

A helping hand

The Pilgrims settled on land occupied by the Native American **Wampanoag Tribe**. Chief Massasoit, head of the tribe, sent men to meet the group. When they saw the Pilgrims were struggling, the tribe taught them how to grow corn, as well as where to fish and hunt.

Roughly 35 million people around the world are descended from the Pilgrims!

Wild turkeys were hunted by the Pilgrims and are still part of traditional Thanksgiving dinners.

The first Thanksgiving

Thanks to the Native Americans' help, the Pilgrims survived the first year in their new home. In the fall of 1621, they harvested the crops they had grown and invited chief Massasoit and the Wampanoag People to **share their feast**—it was the first Thanksgiving.

every year on the fourth Thursday of November.

The journey of an **undercover** botanist

This brilliant botanist **disguised** herself as a man, and became the first woman to sail around the world.

Jeanne Baret

Philibert Commerson

> A botanist is a scientist who studies plants.

Budding botanist

Jeanne Baret worked as a housekeeper for the French botanist Philibert Commerson, but her real **passion was plants**. In the 1760s, explorer Louis-Antoine de Bougainville invited Commerson to join him on a scientific voyage. Commerson wanted to bring Jeanne, but, at the time, women were **banned** from French navy ships.

Louis-Antoine de Bougainville

Baret became the first woman to circumnavigate

I discovered a bright flower in Brazil and named it Bougainvillea, after Captain Bougainville.

Bougainvillea

South America

A man's world

The pair came up with a plan to sneak Baret on board. She **disguised herself as a man** and went by the name Jean. When they reached **South America**, they spent years collecting and classifying hundreds of types of plants.

Female first

Most women at the time never got the chance to leave their village, but Baret broke the law to achieve her dreams. She made history by going all the way **around the world** and making huge contributions to botany. Sadly, she did not get the credit she deserved for hundreds of years.

the globe without even trying to make history!

Call of the **wild**

The Humboldt penguin and Humboldt squid are named after me!

Alexander von Humboldt

This German scientist followed his dreams, before putting pen to paper to give future scientists the greatest **gift** they could hope for.

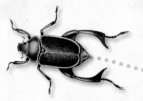

Natural world

In the late 18th century scientists began exploring new lands to find unknown animals and plants. As a child, **Alexander von Humboldt** dreamed of seeing the world, and spent his time **collecting plants, insects, and shells**. He knew he would make studying nature his life's work.

Aimé Bonpland

Alexander von Humboldt

American adventures

In 1799, Humboldt set sail for **South America** with the French botanist **Aimé Bonpland**. They spent five years exploring and finding new lands, plants, and animals.

To do list:

☑ Climb Mount Chimborazo in Ecuador

☑ Map more than 1,700 miles (2,740 km) of the Orinoco River

☑ Found thousands of new species of plants and animals

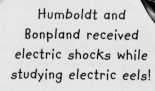

Humboldt and Bonpland received electric shocks while studying electric eels!

Charles Darwin called Humboldt, "the greatest scientific traveler who ever lived."

Prolific writer

In 1804, Humboldt traveled to Paris, France, where he spent the next 20 years writing down his scientific findings. He had collected enough data for **34 volumes**! These documents inspired other young scientists, including Charles Darwin, to continue his work.

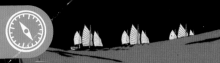

The pirate **queen**

The leader of an enormous army of pirate ships, **Ching Shih** was the most powerful and feared woman on the sea.

Ching Shih →

Setting sail

In 1801, Ching Shih married Zheng Yi, a Chinese pirate lord in charge of a group of ships called the **Red Flag Fleet**. But, before she became his wife, she made sure she would get an equal share of her husband's wealth and power.

Very little is known about Ching Shih—even her name is a mystery. "Ching Shih" means "widow of Ching."

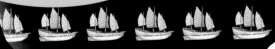

Ching Shih has been called the most

The Terror of South China

When her husband died, Ching Shih became the **sole ruler** of the fleet. She was a strict leader, with a long list of rules for pirates to obey. This made her a powerful pirate queen, who frequently defeated attacks from the government.

Ching Shih ruled more than 1,800 ships, and up to 70,000 pirates!

Happy retirement

In 1810, Ching Shih was forced to give herself up to the Chinese government. She cleverly negotiated with the emperor and was allowed to retire from piracy as a free woman and open a gambling house. She is remembered as the **most feared** pirate queen in Chinese history.

successful pirate in history.

Mapping Australia

This **forgotten hero** was the first Australian to sail all the way around the island, and was instrumental in putting his homeland on the map.

Bungaree

Matthew Flinders

In his memoirs, Flinders wrote about Bungaree's affection and kindness toward the ship's cat, Trim.

The explorers

British Captain **Matthew Flinders** is famous for circumnavigating and mapping Australia at the beginning of the 19th century. However, his Aboriginal Australian guide, **Bungaree**, is lesser known. In 1798, the two explorers met on a voyage to an island off the coast of Australia and became friends.

Bungaree was a born entertainer who loved doing impersonations to amuse audiences.

An epic journey

In 1802, Flinders invited Bungaree aboard merchant ship, *HMS Investigator*. They set off from Sydney on a voyage around **Australia**. As the only native Australian on the ship, Bungaree's knowledge proved invaluable. When tensions grew with indigenous people along the coastline, Bungaree stepped in to defuse the situation. During the year-long trip he served as a friend, interpreter, and diplomat, and became the first Australian to circumnavigate Australia.

Sydney

Making their mark

This epic expedition was important because the entire Australian coastline was recorded, including previously unmapped waters. Flinders and Bungaree's voyage resulted in the first **complete map** of Australia.

An American adventure

In 1803, the US government bought an area of land called the Louisiana Territory from France. Not much was known about the land, so an army captain named **Meriwether Lewis** was sent to check it out.

Hitting the road

Lewis asked his friend, Lieutenant **William Clark**, to go with him. Lewis and Clark got a group of volunteers together and left St. Louis, Missouri, **heading west**. Their goals were to explore the area, find a path to the Pacific Ocean, set up trade routes, and make contact with native people in the area.

On the road

The journey was full of dangers. Many people became sick, others were attacked by ferocious **grizzly bears**, and there were some fights with Native Americans.

William Clark

Meriwether Lewis

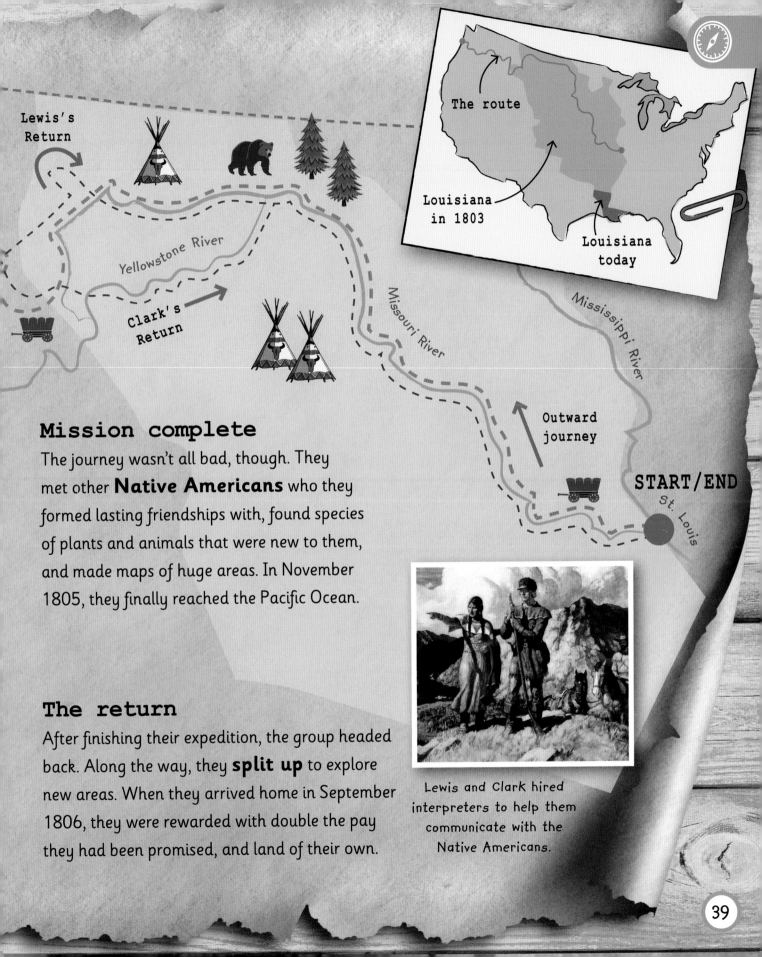

The route

Louisiana in 1803

Louisiana today

Lewis's Return

Clark's Return

Yellowstone River

Missouri River

Mississippi River

Outward journey

START/END

St. Louis

Mission complete

The journey wasn't all bad, though. They met other **Native Americans** who they formed lasting friendships with, found species of plants and animals that were new to them, and made maps of huge areas. In November 1805, they finally reached the Pacific Ocean.

The return

After finishing their expedition, the group headed back. Along the way, they **split up** to explore new areas. When they arrived home in September 1806, they were rewarded with double the pay they had been promised, and land of their own.

Lewis and Clark hired interpreters to help them communicate with the Native Americans.

Leading the way

Lewis and Clark's famous expedition would not have been possible without the help of a particular person: a Native American woman named **Sacagawea**.

In addition to helping Lewis and Clark, Sacagawea spent the trip taking care of her baby!

The pilot

Lewis and Clark knew they would need a guide and translator to help them explore the Louisiana Territory. Sacagawea was the perfect person. Clark called her the team's "**pilot**" because she had deep knowledge of the land and could help them communicate with the Native Americans they met.

Family reunion

At one point on the journey, Sacagawea was sent to speak with a local chief. It turned out to be Chief Cameahwait, her long-lost **brother**! He gave her some horses to help the expedition on its journey.

Sacagawea belonged to the Shoshone Tribe.

Lewis

Clark

Lewis and Clark were so grateful for Sacagawea's heroics, they named the river after her!

To the rescue

Sacagawea's knowledge of the area and her interpreting skills were vital. But she was key to the expedition's success in other ways. While traveling along a river, the rough waters almost capsized the group's boat. Sacagawea **dived into the water** to save important items such as maps and medicine.

The lost city

The location of the lost city of Petra remained a **mystery** to much of the world for more than 1,000 years, until it was finally rediscovered.

City of stone

Petra is an ancient city sculpted from stone. It was the capital city of the Nabataean Kingdom, built in what is now Jordan in about 300 BCE. Petra thrived for centuries as a trading center, but after being badly damaged by earthquakes, the city was **abandoned** in 663 CE.

The stunning backdrop of pink sandstone cliffs earned Petra the nickname "The Rose City."

The Nabataeans were skilled craftspeople and architects who built exquisite homes and beautiful gardens.

Into the rock

Petra is made of beautiful buildings carved into **steep cliffs**. The word Petra comes from the Greek word for rock. The ancient site is full of tombs, temples, houses, and historic monuments.

Found again

In 1812, Swiss explorer **Johann Ludwig Burckhardt** became the first outsider to rediscover the secret city. Petra is surrounded by mountains, and can only be reached via a small canyon, called **Al Siq**, which is why it remained hidden for so long.

The vast majority of Petra is still underground and untouched.

Al Siq

Arctic
opponents

Mystery surrounds the race to reach the North Pole. **Two explorers** have both claimed to be the first to reach the northernmost point on Earth.

> Who was really the first to reach the North Pole?

The path to the North

Many explorers had long set their sights on reaching the North Pole. But this destination was **full of danger**. There were freezing temperatures, shifting ice, strong winds, and devastating storms. Many challengers lost their lives on the way to this remote region, so who would be the first to finally reach it?

NORTH POLE

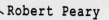
Robert Peary

> I have a photo to prove I got there first.

Frederick Cook

> But I got there a year earlier!

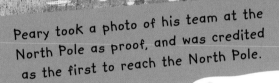
Peary took a photo of his team at the North Pole as proof, and was credited as the first to reach the North Pole.

Peary's persistence

Starting in 1891, American explorer **Robert Peary** tried to reach the North Pole on three separate expeditions. And in another Arctic exploration mission, he suffered frostbite and lost eight toes. But in April 1909, he finally claimed to have made it, along with his assistant, **Matthew Henson**, and four **Inuit companions**.

Matthew Henson

Contenders

When Peary returned, he discovered that fellow American explorer **Frederick Cook** claimed he had been to the North Pole a year earlier, but neither account can be totally confirmed. Some experts doubt Peary arrived first because the details of his journey seem impossible, and Cook has been accused of fraud because his claim came a year later. The truth may never be known, but the first confirmed arrival was when American explorer **Ralph Plaisted** arrived in 1968 by snowmobile.

> In recent years, people have used planes, airships, and even a submarine to reach the North Pole.

Race to the South Pole

The race to reach the **coldest place on Earth** resulted in a historic victory for one brave explorer, while his beaten rival paid the ultimate price.

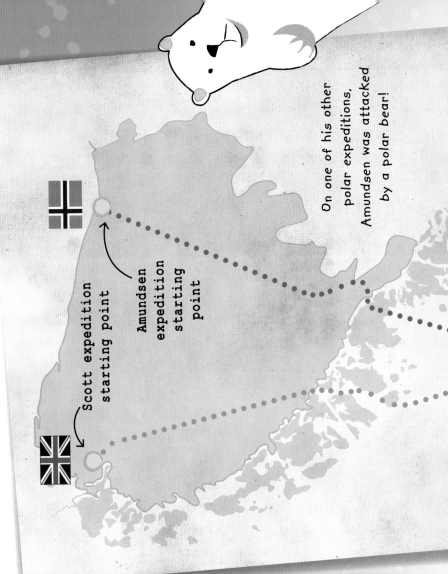

Scott expedition starting point

Amundsen expedition starting point

On one of his other polar expeditions, Amundsen was attacked by a polar bear!

Frozen wilderness

Traveling to Antarctica, the coldest, driest, and windiest place on Earth, presents many challenges. Despite this, reaching the South Pole became the **ultimate goal** for many explorers in the early 20th century, and in 1911, two teams set off for the **South Pole**, taking two different routes.

Race on the ice

Norwegian explorer **Roald Amundsen** set off with four men, four dogsleds, and 52 dogs. Around the same time, British explorer **Robert Falcon Scott** also took four men, who dragged their supplies behind them. Both teams struggled for weeks, overcoming treacherous glaciers, slippery ice sheets, and freezing temperatures.

Historic win

On December 14, 1911, Amundsen arrived at the South Pole and planted the Norwegian flag. Scott arrived on January 17, 1912 only to realize he had been beaten. Amundsen and his team got back to base camp safely, but the on the return trip, bad weather and challenging conditions sadly cost Scott and his men their lives.

Amundsen's advantage

Amundsen's team adopted survival techniques used by Inuit people. They wore animal furs to keep warm and the dogs pulled the heavy sleds to lighten their load. Scott's men may have lost the race and their lives, but they remain **brave heroes** of exploration.

It took 99 days for Amundsen's team to reach the South Pole and return safely to base camp.

→ Roald Amundsen

South Pole

Scott's team

47

Trapped
in the ice

During the age of polar exploration, this **brave adventurer** led an expedition unlike any other and became a hero.

Ernest Shackleton

Aborted attempts

Irish explorer Ernest Shackleton was on a mission to be the first person to **reach the South Pole**. He went on expeditions in 1901 and 1908, but had to abandon them. These adventures, however, led to a lifelong obsession with Antarctica.

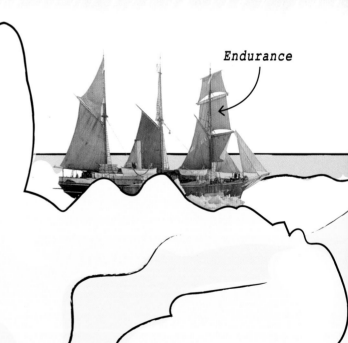

Endurance

Shackleton's family motto was "BY ENDURANCE WE CONQUER."

A new plan

In 1911, when Norwegian explorer Roald Amundsen became the first person to reach the South Pole, Shackleton set himself a new goal. His plan was to cross the entire continent of Antarctica via the South Pole. In 1914, he and a crew of 28 set off on board the ship **Endurance**.

Lifeboats' journey to Elephant Island

Endurance trapped in the ice

START

SEA ICE

South Pole

ANTARCTICA

— Shackleton's route in 1908

— Amundsen's route in 1911

— Shackleton's route in 1914-1916

Doomed voyage

Endurance became **stuck in the ice** for 10 months and sank. The crew used floating ice and lifeboats to reach Elephant Island. From there, Shackleton led five of the crew on a rescue mission through stormy seas and across mountains. Their heroics led to every one of the crew surviving.

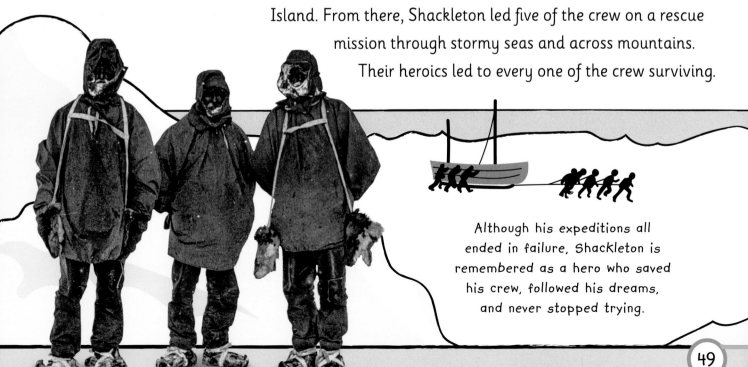

Although his expeditions all ended in failure, Shackleton is remembered as a hero who saved his crew, followed his dreams, and never stopped trying.

The period known as ancient Egypt is remembered for many things, including royals known as "pharaohs."

The tomb of **King Tut**

In 1917, a team of archaeologists set out to find the tomb of an ancient Egyptian pharaoh—a "boy king" known as **Tutankhamen**, or King Tut.

Howard Carter

The mysterious king

Little was known about Tut before 1922, and many experts believed his tomb would never be found. But British archaeologist **Howard Carter** disagreed and launched a dig in the Valley of the Kings, Egypt.

The secret staircase

Carter and his team spent six years in search of a major discovery without much luck. But, in 1922, they stumbled upon a hidden staircase. After it was cleared, they **uncovered** a door, and behind it was the undisturbed burial chamber of the boy king!

Treasure

Buried treasure

Inside the chamber lay thousands of items that had remained **unseen** for over 3,000 years. Many were cast in gold and beautifully decorated. And inside a golden coffin lay the remains of King Tut. Since the discovery, King Tut has become one of the most **famous** ancient Egyptian pharaohs.

Trek to the top

In 1953, Edmund Hillary and Tenzing Norgay did what many before them had tried and failed to do. They climbed to the top of **Mount Everest**—the highest mountain on Earth.

Hillary

New Zealand's Edmund Hillary fell in love with snow and climbing after going on a school skiing trip when he was 16. Just four years later, he climbed New Zealand's Mount Ollivier, and later scaled Mount Cook, the highest mountain in New Zealand. But his **dream** was to climb Mount Everest in Nepal.

Norgay

Norgay grew up near the Himalayas and started climbing at a young age. Years before meeting Hillary, he carried equipment on mountaineering expeditions, including an attempt to scale Everest in 1935. His experience made him the perfect **partner** for Hillary on their attempt to reach the peak.

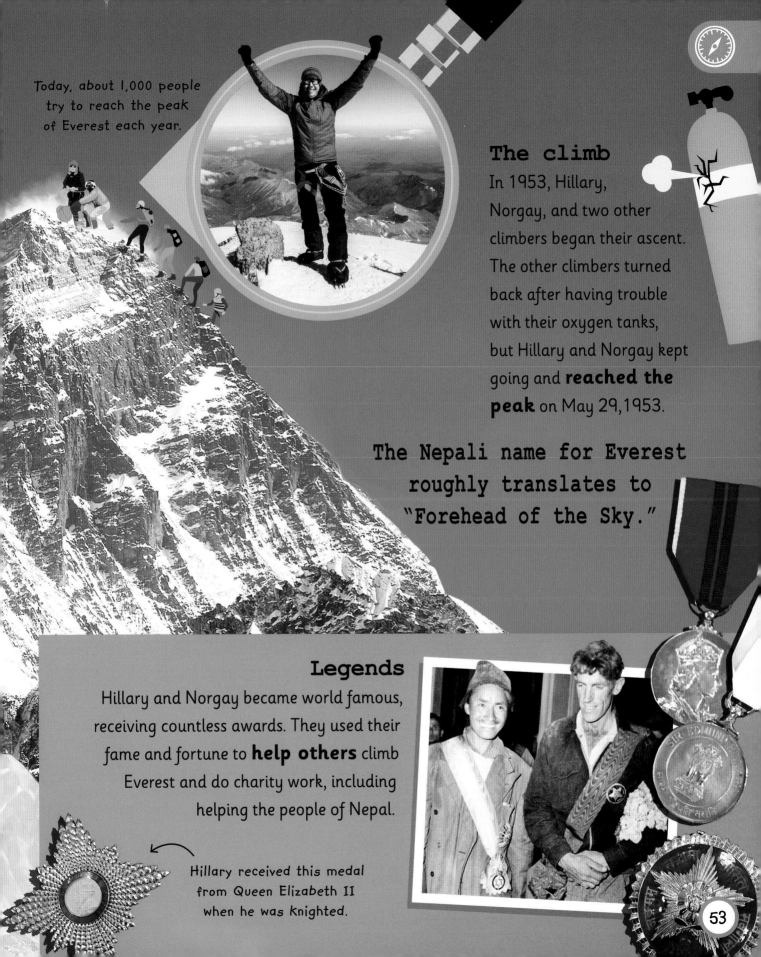

Today, about 1,000 people try to reach the peak of Everest each year.

The climb

In 1953, Hillary, Norgay, and two other climbers began their ascent. The other climbers turned back after having trouble with their oxygen tanks, but Hillary and Norgay kept going and **reached the peak** on May 29, 1953.

The Nepali name for Everest roughly translates to "Forehead of the Sky."

Legends

Hillary and Norgay became world famous, receiving countless awards. They used their fame and fortune to **help others** climb Everest and do charity work, including helping the people of Nepal.

Hillary received this medal from Queen Elizabeth II when he was knighted.

The first person in space

During the 1950s and 60s, the US and Soviet Union were in a race to send a person into space. This dangerous mission would require a remarkable person who was physically fit, brave, and could stay calm under pressure. Enter **Yuri Gagarin**.

Vostok 1

Top choice

The Russians finished building a special craft for the mission called **Vostok 1**, but they needed someone to fly in it. After testing 154 people, they chose a young pilot, Yuri Gagarin.

To get ready for the mission, Yuri had to train as hard as an Olympic athlete.

The launch

On April 12, 1961, Vostok 1 **blasted off** with Gagarin on board. Parts of Vostok 1 were designed to break away as it got higher—this made it lighter. After about 10 minutes, Yuri was alone in a special capsule traveling around Earth. They had done it!

Vostok 1 capsule

The return

Yuri spent 108 minutes orbiting the Earth, talking on the radio to his support team. When it was time to go back, engines fired and sent the capsule back to Earth. Yuri ejected and parachuted to safety in Kazakhstan.

Gagarin remains one of Russia's greatest heroes. A statue in his honor was built in the capital city of Moscow.

Earth

Mission to the **moon**

People have long wondered what it would be like to travel to another planet. Nobody has done it yet, but in 1969, three brave men did the **next best thing**.

Project Apollo

Throughout the 1960s, NASA was working hard on the **Apollo Program**—a project with the goal of landing on the moon. By mid-1969, it had launched a series of Apollo missions—but none had taken people to the moon.

Saturn V

Lift off!

In July 1969, the Apollo 11 mission was launched by the Saturn V rocket from the Kennedy Space Center in Florida, US. It was a dangerous mission, but there were three willing astronauts on board—**Neil Armstrong**, **Edwin "Buzz" Aldrin**, and **Michael Collins**.

"That's one small step for a man, one giant leap for mankind."
—Neil Armstrong

Lunar lander

Buzz Aldrin

Neil Armstrong

One small step

After four days, the lunar lander set down on the moon. Neil Armstrong, the mission commander, became the **first person** to set foot on the moon. He described the ground as being "almost like a powder." Buzz Aldrin joined him and they took pictures and collected rock and soil samples while Michael Collins waited in orbit.

The return

After spending less than 22 hours on the moon, the men began their return trip to Earth. The three astronauts were welcomed home as **heroes** for their amazing and historic achievement.

Apollo 11 splashed down in the Pacific Ocean.

Uncovering the terra-cotta army

In 1974, farmers digging a well in Xi'an, China, stumbled across an amazing discovery: **ancient statues** of soldiers buried underground. These helped historians learn about the China of the past and the life of its first emperor.

The stone soldiers and horses were built to

After the farmers made the first discovery, archaeologists arrived to examine the dig site. It turned out that there were a lot more statues—more than **8,000**. An entire army of them!

There were statues of soldiers, chariots, and even horses. Historians figured out they were built more than 2,200 years earlier to protect the tomb of China's first emperor and guard him in the **afterlife**.

This "terra-cotta army" turned out to be one of the most important archaeological discoveries ever, and is sometimes called the "Eighth Wonder of the World."

Archaeologists have spent years excavating the statues. They think workers spent 30 years building them!

Each statue is incredibly detailed. They have different facial features, carried real weapons, and were once painted bright colors.

I renamed myself "Qin Shi Huang," which means "first emperor."

protect the EMPEROR'S TOMB.

China used to be split into different states, but in 221 BCE the leader of one of these states, **King Zheng**, conquered the others and unified China as one country.

Zheng wanted his achievements to last **forever**. He had a huge tomb built with a stone army to protect it, so he could continue to rule from the afterlife.

Outback
adventure

The Australian desert is a dangerous place with soaring temperatures, little water, and deadly wildlife. **Robyn Davidson** knew all this when she set herself the challenge of a solo crossing.

Adventurous spirit

Robyn Davidson was born in Australia in 1950. Her childhood home was near a creek and she used to pretend it was the Amazon River. Her early **dreams of adventure** would surely one day become a reality.

Diggity

Camel Lady

In 1977, the so-called **Camel Lady** set off with four camels and her pet dog, Diggity. They trekked for nine months through the deserts of Western Australia. Robyn stayed on course by checking maps and following the stars.

Australia

Start

Finish

Robyn spent time learning from Aboriginal Australians about how to stay alive in the desert.

At the end of the journey, Robyn and her camels finally reached the Indian Ocean and jumped in for a swim!

Camels are called "ships of the desert" because they're adapted for desert life.

Always wandering

Robyn wrote a best-selling book about her adventure, and has continued to **write** and **travel**. Much of her writing is about the lives of **nomadic people**, who travel from place to place rather than living in one spot.

The peak of success

There was no mountain high enough to stop this courageous climber from **reaching the top**!

A head for heights

Austrian adventurer **Gerlinde Kaltenbrunner** was born in 1970. She grew up surrounded by mountains, where she learned to trek and ski. Climbing became her main interest, and as a teenager she started scaling mountains in the Alps, the highest range in Europe, before setting her sights on a bigger challenge.

At just 13 years old, Kaltenbrunner climbed Sturzhahn, an Austrian mountain measuring 6,654 ft (2,028 m) in height.

Shishapangma
26,335 ft (8,027 m)

Gasherbrum II

Broad Peak

Gasherbrum I

Annapurna I

Nanga Parbat

Manaslu

All 14 mountains taller than 26,250ft (8,000m)

Everest

Problem peak

Earth has 14 mountains measuring more than 26,250 ft (8,000 m), and Kaltenbrunner was determined to climb them all. Although Mount Everest in Nepal is the tallest, **K2** in Pakistan proved to be most difficult. It took her seven attempts to reach the top!

"K2 was my most wonderful, but also my most difficult expedition by far."
—Gerlinde Kaltenbrunner

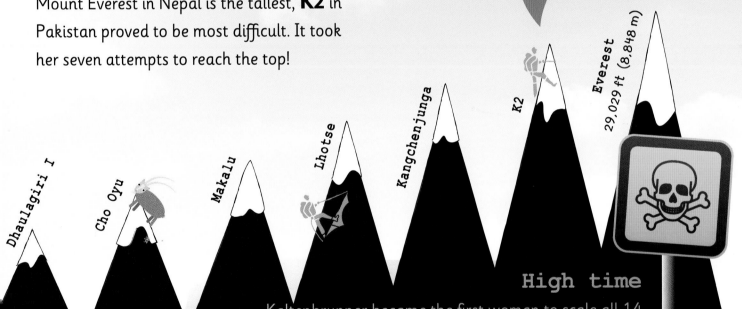

Dhaulagiri I

Cho Oyu

Makalu

Lhotse

Kangchenjunga

K2

Everest
29,029 ft (8,848 m)

High time

Kaltenbrunner became the first woman to scale all 14 peaks without an oxygen tank. In 2012, she won an Explorer of the Year award. Although she has vowed never to return to these major mountains, she still enjoys climbing and skiing in the Alps.

are located in the Himalayas in Asia.

Diving director

Of all the unexplored places in the world, the seas and oceans are the biggest. Yet, one man managed to reach the deepest underwater spot on Earth: the **Mariana Trench**.

James Cameron

Ocean exploration

Canadian movie director **James Cameron** is best known for making hit movies, but he's also a deep-sea explorer. Along with a team of experts, he constructed a special submarine that could withstand the huge pressure of the deep water—they named it *Deepsea Challenger*.

Deepsea Challenger

Solo descent

In 2012, *Deepsea Challenger* was lowered into the **Pacific Ocean** over the Mariana Trench. James was the only person inside. His compass didn't work correctly, and the sonar system died, but his vertical diving vehicle reached the deepest point on Earth in just over two and a half hours.

James spent a lot of time underwater while shooting movies such as *Titanic* and *The Abyss*.

A Cuvier's beaked whale can dive deeper than any other animal. It can reach depths of 9,784 ft (2,992 m)—but that's nowhere near as deep as the Mariana Trench!

Incredible achievement

Once at the bottom, James spent three hours taking photos and gathering samples, before returning safely to the surface. In addition to achieving the record for the **deepest solo dive ever**, James inspired people across the globe to embrace ocean exploration.

The world's tallest tower, Burj Khalifa, is 2,716 ft (828 m) tall.

The world's tallest tower would need to be stacked on top of itself 13 times to reach the depth of the Mariana Trench.

Deepsea Challenger

The Mariana Trench is at a depth of 35,756 feet (10,994 m).

Scientists and

inventors

Imagine making a discovery that has the power to change the world, or developing a new medicine that could save millions of lives. Turn the page to meet the people whose ingenious ideas and incredible achievements **changed the course** of history.

Mathematical
mastermind

EUREKA!!!

Archimedes is most famous for a bright idea at **bath time**, but he is also remembered for a lifetime of brilliant calculations and inspiring inventions.

Royal request

Archimedes was born in ancient Greece in about 288 BCE. He soon developed a love of math and word spread of his genius. King Hiero II asked Archimedes to solve a very tricky problem—to figure out if the royal crown was made from a bar of **pure gold**, or if the goldsmith had mixed in some silver.

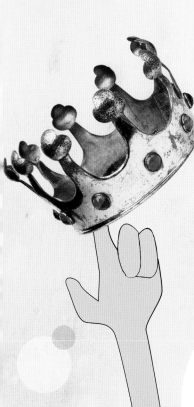

Bathing brilliance

Archimedes couldn't solve it, until one day he stepped into a bath and saw the water overflow. Legend has it he jumped out of the bath shouting "**Eureka**!" ("I've found it!"). He realized that if the crown was really made from a bar of pure gold, if he put it in water it would shift the exact same amount of water as a bar of gold, but it didn't!

A crater on the moon is named after Archimedes.

Archimedes catapult

Lasting legacy

Archimedes continued to dream up new ideas and **inventions** such as a type of catapult, and a pulley that is still used today.

Although Archimedes was a math whiz, he also loved poetry, art, and music.

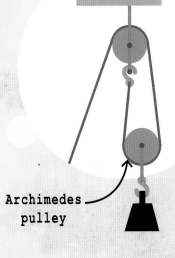

Archimedes pulley

69

Printing pioneer

Imagine writing huge books by hand. Now imagine doing it over and over again. That's what used to happen before German inventor **Johannes Gutenberg** created a printing press to do the hard work.

Ingenious invention

Gutenberg's printer worked by pressing a piece of paper onto inked letter blocks. His invention made making books much **quicker** than writing them by hand, but he had to borrow money to build it.

Letter block

Johannes Gutenberg

Block printing was first used in Asia, almost 600 years before Gutenberg's printer.

Gutenberg printing press

Printing revolution

Made in 1455 using the Gutenberg printing press, **the Gutenberg Bible** was the first book to be **mass-produced** (made in large quantities). Thanks to Gutenberg, ideas could be replicated quickly and shared more widely.

Gutenberg Bible

Printer and the pauper

Although his invention changed the world, Gutenberg **never made any money** from it. He could not repay his debts so his business was taken over by the man who lent him the money. Even though Gutenberg continued making books, his name was never printed in them.

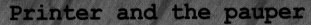

71

Imprisoned **astronomer**

This brilliant scientist made discoveries that would **change the course of history**. Not everybody, however, liked hearing what he had to say...

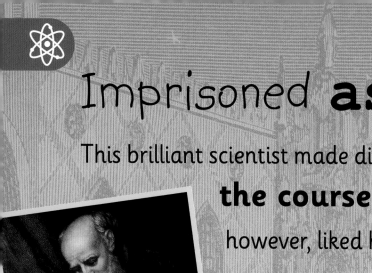

Galileo
Galilei

Seeing stars

Italian scientist Galileo Galilei was born in 1564, during a time of invention and discovery. He took interest in the **telescope**, which had been invented to study enemy ships, and designed his own version that he used to study space.

Galileo made his mark on the world time and time again, and is one of history's greatest scientists.

Galileo saw craters on the moon...

...the moons around Jupiter...

...and so much more.

Different thinking

At the time, Earth was considered the center of the universe, but a Polish astronomer, **Nicolaus Copernicus**, believed that planets moved around the sun. After observing Mercury and Venus circling the sun, Galileo realized that Copernicus was right and the Earth does as well.

Galileo at his home.

Changing minds

The discovery was truly revolutionary. Earth not being the center of the universe was difficult for people to accept, and went against religious teachings. Galileo was ordered not to write about his discovery, but he did anyway. Although he was later proven to be right, he was arrested and put under **house arrest** for the rest of his life. Galileo had to stay imprisoned in his house. Although he couldn't leave, he was allowed visitors, including poets and philosophers.

Astronomical **adventure**

Comets have appeared in the night sky throughout human history, but we didn't know much about them before **Edmond Halley's** big discovery.

Mastermind

Edmond Halley was an English astronomer and mathematician born in 1656. Obsessed with math and science from a young age, Halley was fascinated by **comets** and spent a lot of time studying them.

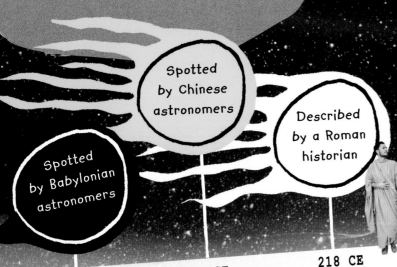

Spotted by Babylonian astronomers

Spotted by Chinese astronomers

Described by a Roman historian

164 BCE

12 BCE

218 CE

1066 CE

1301 CE

Recorded on the Bayeux Tapestry

Using Halley's discovery, we can look back in time and track Halley's Comet through human history.

Painted by an Italian artist

74

A comet's return

After having read reports of comets in 1531 and 1607, when he saw one in 1682 he realized it was actually the same comet showing up again and again. He figured out the comet also orbited the sun, and every **75-76** years its journey crossed paths with Earth.

Sun

Earth

Predicting the future

As Halley predicted, the comet returned in 1758. Halley died in 1742, so sadly never got to see it again. The comet is, however, now named **Halley's Comet** in his honor.

Seen by Halley

Photographed for the first time

Next return of Halley's comet!

1682 CE   1758 CE   1910 CE   1986 CE   2061 CE

Reappears, proving Halley right

Last seen from Earth

Groundbreaking
botanist

Fascinated with plants and nature, Swedish scientist and traveler **Carl Linnaeus**, made an enormous impact in the world of botany.

Botany is the scientific study of plants—from the smallest flowers to the most enormous trees!

Studying botany

In Carl Linnaeus's time, most medicines were plant based. Carl decided to become a **doctor**, so during his time at college, he was able to delve into his true passion—botany.

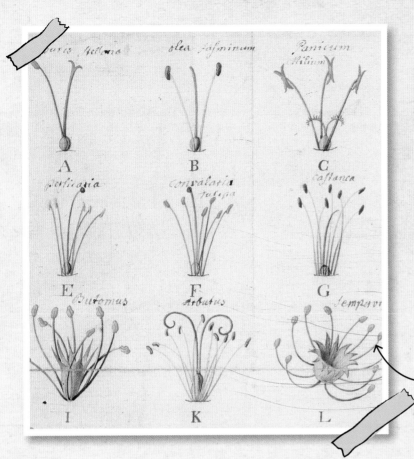

Diverse discoveries

Carl went on trips to Lapland and around Sweden, where he recorded all the plants he found. He worked hard to put plants into **categories**, using a two-part naming system which he invented. In 1735, Carl published his first book, *Systema Naturae*.

In Linnaeus's book, plants and animals were ordered according to how similar they were.

Taken from Systema Naturae

Carl named useless WEEDS after people he didn't like!

Top of the class

After becoming a teacher, Carl and his students went on more trips to find new types of plants. The first edition of his book was only **12 pages long**, but they found so many plants that the 12th edition was **2,400 pages**! Carl's system of **ordering plants**, as well as animals, is still the system we use today.

Linnaeus classifying plants in his garden in Sweden.

Bright spark

Flying a kite on a windy day can be a lot of fun. But this American **electricity** enthusiast risked his life flying a kite in thunder and lightning to prove his groundbreaking theories.

Bookworm

Born in 1706, **Benjamin Franklin** was the youngest son in a family of 17 children. He didn't receive much education, but loved books, and gained a wealth of knowledge from reading, especially in science.

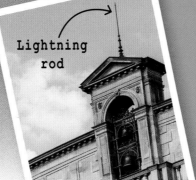

Lightning rod

Franklin playing the armonica

Perfect storm

One stormy day in 1752, Franklin went outside and flew a kite with a metal key attached to it by string. Despite the pouring rain, deafening thunder, and lightning strikes, Franklin noticed sparks flying off the key. It was a dangerous experiment, but it proved that **lightning** is a form of electricity.

Inventions and influence

Franklin's work with lightning resulted in him inventing the **lightning rod**, which protects buildings against lightning strikes. But he was a man of many talents who dreamed up other innovations, including an instrument called the **armonica**, a metal-lined stove, and bifocal glasses!

Franklin was also celebrated for a series of groundbreaking firsts, including helping found the first library in the US and establishing the first university in Pennsylvania.

Franklin appears on $100 bills in America.

The mother of **computing**

The first mechanical computer that could perform calculations was designed by British inventor Charles Babbage. However, the first person to understand it could do so much more was **Ada Lovelace**.

What a fascinating machine!

Ada Lovelace

Meeting Babbage

Ada was born in 1815. She was very intelligent and studied mathematics and science, subjects that most women were not allowed to study at the time. In 1833, one of Ada's teachers introduced her to **Charles Babbage**, and they soon became friends.

The analytical engine

Babbage had designed computing machines: a difference engine, which performed basic mathematical functions, and an analytical engine, which handled more complicated calculations. An Italian engineer, Luigi Federico Menabrea, wrote an article about the analytical engine. Charles asked Ada to **translate** it.

Ada, can you translate this for me please?

Charles Babbage

Analytical engine

NOTES

Ada's notes

When Ada translated the article, she had added her own plans about how the machine could be programmed to do things. Many people consider this the first computer program, and Ada the first **computer programmer**. The second Tuesday of every October is celebrated as Ada Lovelace Day.

Later in life, Ada thought she could use her mathematical skills to help her win at gambling, but the plan didn't work.

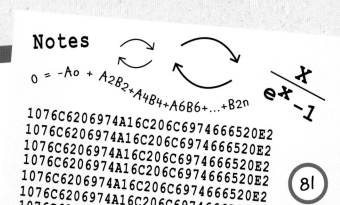

Notes

$$0 = -A_0 + A_2B_2 + A_4B_4 + A_6B_6 + \ldots + B_{2n}$$

$$\frac{x}{e^x - 1}$$

1076C6206974A16C206C6974666520E2
1076C6206974A16C206C6974666520E2
1076C6206974A16C206C6974666520E2
1076C6206974A16C206C6974666520E2
1076C6206974A16C206C6974666520E2
1076C6206974A16C206C6974666520E2
1076C6206974A16C206C6974666520E2
1076C6206974A16C206C6974666520E2
1076C6206074

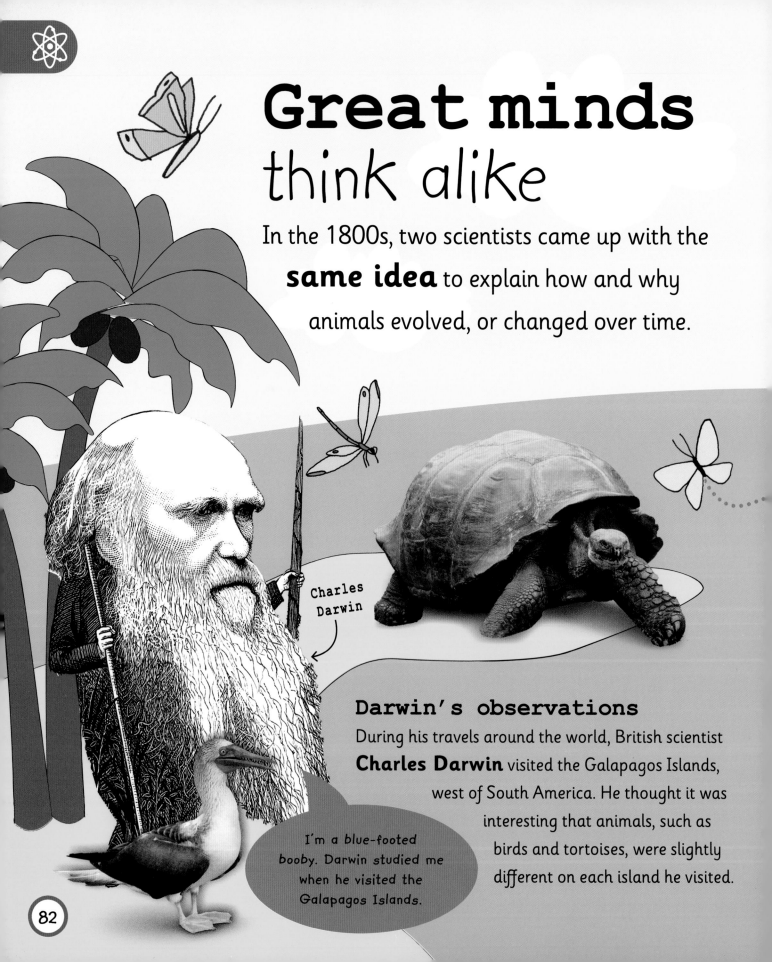

Great minds think alike

In the 1800s, two scientists came up with the **same idea** to explain how and why animals evolved, or changed over time.

Charles Darwin

Darwin's observations

During his travels around the world, British scientist **Charles Darwin** visited the Galapagos Islands, west of South America. He thought it was interesting that animals, such as birds and tortoises, were slightly different on each island he visited.

I'm a blue-footed booby. Darwin studied me when he visited the Galapagos Islands.

A new idea

When Charles returned home, he came up with a new theory of evolution (how living things change over time), which he called **natural selection**. He started to write a book about it.

Charles noticed that finches living in different areas of the Galapagos Islands were related, but had slightly different beaks, which helped each species survive in its own environment.

Though they did not agree on everything, the two men admired and respected each other very much.

Wallace's findings

Meanwhile, another British explorer named **Alfred Russel Wallace** was in Indonesia, Southeast Asia. He noticed two islands were home to completely different animals and plants, even though they were very close together.

A shared discovery

Charles spent years writing his book and keeping his theories to himself, but in 1858, Alfred wrote to Charles about an idea he wanted to publish. Charles realized that they had made the **same discovery**, and it was time to publish his book and share their theory with the world.

Alfred
Wallace

The discovery of **dynamite**

This scientist set the world alight with his explosive inventions, but in the end **peace** became his lasting legacy.

Dynamite takes its name from the Greek word for "power."

Explosive experiments

During the 1850s, Swedish teenager **Alfred Nobel** was studying chemical engineering and became very interested in explosives. At the time, explosives were very unstable, and Alfred wanted to make them safer. In 1867 he succeeded by inventing **dynamite**.

I hope this invention helps a lot of people.

A deadly development

Dynamite replaced **gunpowder** as a safer explosive for
mining, blasting tunnels, and building roads and railroads.
Alfred became very rich, but there was a downside—dynamite
also became a weapon of war.

A glimpse of the future

Alfred was shocked one day, when he read about
his own death in a newspaper! The article had
been printed by mistake, but claimed dynamite
made him rich while making others suffer, and
called him **"The Merchant of Death."**
Alfred didn't want to be remembered for this, and
decided to change his legacy.

DAILY NEWS

THE MERCHANT
OF DEATH

Nobel Prize

Pioneer of peace

When Alfred really died, he left his riches to help set up
a yearly award for achievements in physics, chemistry,
medicine, literature, and peace that would benefit mankind.
In 1901 the **Nobel Prize** was launched. To this day, it
remains among the most important awards in the world.

Top scientist

Winning a Nobel Prize is one of the greatest honors in the world. **Marie Curie** didn't stop at just one—she won two!

A special mind

Marie was born in 1867 in Poland, and moved to Paris to study science. It was there she met her husband, physicist Pierre Curie. Together, they began pioneering work in the scientific field of **radiation**.

Uranium

Radiation is the transmission of energy in the form of waves or particles. Marie studied the rays given off by the newly discovered chemical element uranium.

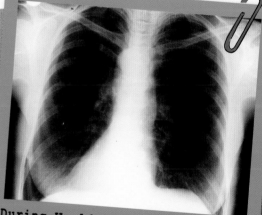

Nobel Prize medals

A scientific partnership

Together, Marie and Pierre discovered two new elements, polonium—which Marie named after her homeland—and radium. In 1903 the Curies were awarded the **Nobel Prize in Physics**. Eight years later, Marie won a second **Nobel Prize in Chemistry**.

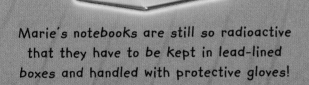

Marie's notebooks are still so radioactive that they have to be kept in lead-lined boxes and handled with protective gloves!

Irène Joliot-Curie

During World War I, Marie helped surgeons x-Ray soldiers for bullets and fractures. She set up mobile X-Ray units, and even drove one herself!

Genius runs in the family. Marie's daughter, Irène, went on to win her own Nobel Prize in Chemistry in 1935.

Lasting legacy

Marie was a rare kind of genius. She was the first woman to win a Nobel Prize, and the first person to win two. Sadly, Marie likely died as a result of her work with dangerous radiation, but her work has helped doctors **save countless lives**.

An accidental stroke of **luck**

Doctors and scientists work very hard to discover new and better ways to treat illnesses. But one of the most important breakthroughs in medical history was discovered completely by **accident!**

Brainy but messy

Scottish scientist **Alexander Fleming** studied bacteria and regularly collected petri dishes of germs taken from tears, saliva, and even snot. Fleming was a brilliant scientist, but he wasn't very good at **cleaning up his laboratory**!

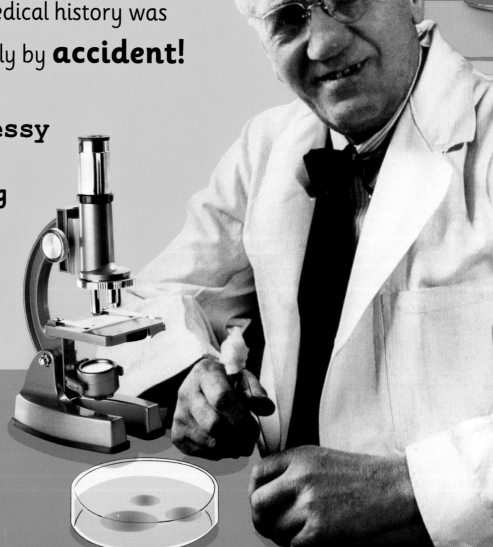

Fantastic fungus

In 1928, when Fleming came back from a two-week vacation, he noticed one of the dirty petri dishes he'd left in the sink had **grown fungus**.

Not only that, the germs that had been in the dish had been killed!

Fungus

Germ

Petri dish

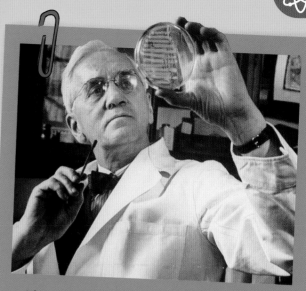

When Fleming studied the fungus, he found it made a special substance that was great at killing germs. He called the substance "penicillin."

A lucky discovery

Fleming had discovered the world's first **antibiotic**. Antibiotics are used to treat all kinds of illnesses that make people sick. Fleming's discovery has saved millions of lives, and is one of history's most important innovations.

A group of scientists, Howard Florey, Ernst Chain, and Norman Heatley, continued Fleming's work by purifying penicillin to make it safe.

Before he decided on the name "penicillin," Fleming called his discovery "mold juice."

Pioneering
programmer

America's **Grace Hopper** led the way for women in computing and made programming easier for everybody.

Grace advertising a user-friendly computer language.

Accessible to all

In 1934, Grace became one of the first women to earn a PhD degree in **mathematics**. During World War II she joined the US Navy and developed a love of computers. After experiencing the difficulties of computer programming, she set out to invent a program of instructions that could be understood by everyone.

Grace once found a moth inside her computer, which led to the term "bug" being used to describe different computer problems.

The annual Celebration of Women in Computing Conference was set

Universal language

Grace developed **FLOW-MATIC**, the first programming language to replace mathematical symbols with familiar English words. It led to computer code becoming simpler, and eventually helped computer users around the world speak the same **computer language**.

Grace using a manual tape-punch computer.

In the Navy, Grace reached the high rank of Rear Admiral. When she retired at age 79, she became the oldest serving officer in the US Armed Forces.

Grace Hopper

Amazing Grace

Grace's achievements and awards earned her the name **"Amazing Grace"** after the famous song. Following her own success, she devoted her time to **training young people** and encouraging them to get into computer programming.

A supercomputer and US naval ship were named *Hopper* in honor of Grace.

HOPPER

up in memory of Grace.

The inventor of instant noodles

This Japanese genius helped feed the world with his **quick-fix foodie favorite**.

Cheap eats

After World War II, money was scarce and food shortages were common. Japanese inventor **Momofuku Ando** thought he might have a solution. After a lot of experimenting, he came up with a method of flash-frying noodles, which made them last a lot longer.

Instant noodles were voted Japan's best invention of the 20th century.

A factory worker holding a box of the first instant noodles.

Instant hit

It wasn't long before these "instant" noodles were popular all over Japan. They were **cheap** to buy, **tasty** to eat, and **easy** to prepare (just add water!). In 1971, a foam container was introduced and "cup noodles" became a worldwide phenomenon.

WOW!

Ando came up with the idea for the cup on a trip to the US, when he spotted customers putting noodles in coffee cups instead of bowls.

Hero to the hungry

Not only had Ando invented the **ultimate convenience food**, he had also helped feed the hungry. The Japanese and American governments were both grateful, and soon awards flooded in—including the 1977 Medal of Honor for his service to the people of Japan.

Momofuku Ando

Ando claimed his good health was due to eating cup noodles. He lived to be 96!

Instant Noodles Just add water

The CupNoodles Museum in Osaka, Japan is dedicated to Ando and his creations.

Connecting the **world**

Every day, huge amounts of **data** travels around the world in the form of emails, text messages, and photos. But none of this would be possible without the work of one man...

Sir Charles Kuen Kao

Bright idea

Charles Kuen Kao was born in China in 1933, and later moved to England to study electrical engineering. In the 1960s, he and his colleagues looked for ways to improve **fiber optics**, a technology that allows data, in the form of light, to be sent over long distances using glass fibers.

In 2009, Charles was awarded the Nobel Prize

The problem

One of the problems with fiber optics at the time was that **signals** sent through existing cables didn't go very far and often died before reaching their destination. Charles studied this problem for a long time.

Glass master

Charles realized there were too many **impurities** in the cables, that slowed down the light which was trying to travel through them—like bumps on a road. He decided to make cables with the **purest glass fiber** he could find.

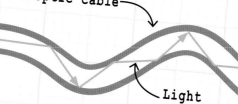

Fiber-optic cable

Light

The light in a fiber-optic cable travels by bouncing along mirror-lined walls until it reaches its destination.

Super solution

This new glass fiber worked incredibl well, and data could now be sent thousands of miles without any proble It wasn't long before fiber-optic cables being **used all over the world**.

Every year, the Nobel Prize is awarded to the most important achievements in various fields.

Nobel Prize

in Physics for his breakthrough.

Margaret and the code her team developed.

Shoot for the **moon**

This cosmic queen of computers helped develop the special **software** needed to put the first humans on the moon.

Starry-eyed scientist

American computer whiz **Margaret Hamilton** always had her eyes on the sky. As a software engineer (a term she came up with), she worked on a computer program to predict weather patterns and spot enemy aircraft. But then NASA got in touch...

Safety first

NASA was working hard to put a person on the moon. Margaret led the team that developed the software for the in-flight computer. She knew safety was very important, so she worked hard on computer code for an **alarm system** that would warn if something was going wrong.

The Presidential Medal of Freedom is the highest honor awarded to a US civilian.

```
LUNAR LANDING GUIDANCE EQUATIONS
- - - - - - - - - - - - - - - - - - - - - - - - - - - - -
REF   45   LAST   799   31,2537   3 4752   0   CAF    TWO
REF    3   LAST   739   31,2540   55,621   1   TS     WCHPHOLD
REF    3   LAST   785   31,2641   55,351   0   TS     WCHPHASE
REF  223   LAST   791   31,2542   0 4616   1   TC     BANKCALL
REF    4   LAST   762   31,2543    40165   1   CADR   STOPRATE
REF   70   LAST   781   31,2544    00311   1   ADRES  XOVINFLAG
REF    3   LAST   229   31,2545   0 5516   0   TC     DOWNFLAG
REF   71   LAST   801   31,2546   0 5516   0   ADRES  REDFLAG
REF    2   LAST   785   31,2547    00143   1   TCF    VERTGUID

REF    3   LAST   800   31,2551   0 5311   1   TC     WCHPHASE

REF  146   LAST   800   31,2553   3 4755   1   CAF
REF    1                31,2554   55,746   1   TS
```

Mission accomplished

In 1969, the world watched the **Apollo 11** mission land safely on the moon. The alarm system turned out to be vital—without it, the landing would have had to be aborted at the last minute. Margaret's pioneering work resulted in her being awarded the Presidential Medal of Freedom in 2016.

Around 400,000 people in total worked to make the mission a success!

Watch this **space**

It's not just people who can go on adventures—the **Voyager space probes** have spent more than 40 years traveling through space and beyond our solar system.

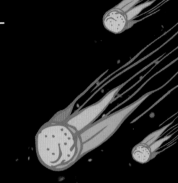

Earth

Planetary studies

In 1977, Voyager 1 and 2 were launched toward **Jupiter** and **Saturn** to study the giant planets. During this planetary tour, the probes captured the stunning detail of Saturn's rings, and discovered three new moons of Saturn and volcanoes on Jupiter's moon, Io.

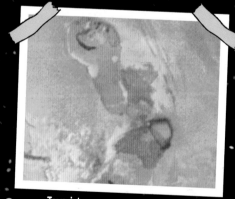

Jupiter

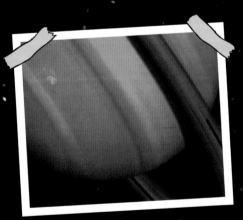

Saturn

Pushing the boundaries

Both probes were so successful that scientists on Earth decided to extend the missions. Voyager 2 reached **Uranus** in 1986 and **Neptune** in 1989, sending incredible images of the planets back to Earth. It's still the only spacecraft to reach these planets.

Voyager 2

Aboard each probe is a special gold record crammed full of pictures, sounds, and greetings in multiple languages from Earth.

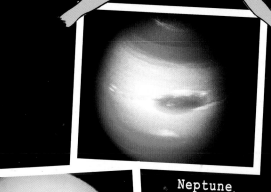

Neptune

Uranus

Interstellar mission

Both probes are currently exploring the universe. In 2012, Voyager 1 traveled **outside the solar system**, and Voyager 2 did the same in 2018. Scientists hope that Voyager 1 and 2 will continue to explore outer space for the next 10 years.

Voyager 1

The Voyager spacecraft were originally built to last only five years!

Mission to **Mars**

There are a lot of humans who have made remarkable journeys. But more and more, **robots** are becoming useful tools for exploration.

Roving around

In 1997, the spacecraft **Pathfinder** landed on Mars. After speeding to the ground, it unfurled a parachute to slow down, and released special air bags to cushion its landing. Two ramps lowered, and out rolled **Sojourner**, the first "rover" to explore Mars' surface.

Pathfinder landed in a region of Mars that had lots of rocks for Sojourner to study. Scientists on Earth looked at the data for clues about how Mars used to be. They believe Mars was once warmer and wetter than it is today.

Mission complete

Sojourner traveled around Mars, gathering **rock samples** and taking photos. It was designed to last seven days, but kept going for almost three months! The information Sojourner gathered was very valuable to scientists, and since then, other rovers have been sent to follow in its footsteps.

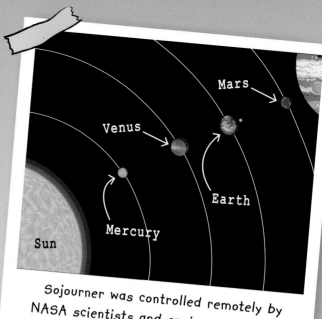

Sojourner was controlled remotely by NASA scientists and engineers on Earth!

Sojourner

Sojourner had two cameras at the front and one at the rear. It used them to snap hundreds of photographs for scientists.

The amazing **machine**

In 2008, scientists from around the world finished building the world's biggest machine in Switzerland. The goal is for the **Large Hadron Collider** (LHC) to solve some of the greatest mysteries in science.

The LHC was built by CERN, an organization made up of some of the best scientists from around the world working together.

The LHC is longer than 260 soccer fields

Inside the LHC

The LHC is the world's biggest, most expensive, and most complicated machine. It allows scientists to crash tiny things called **particles** into each other at almost the **speed of light** to recreate conditions similar to those at the start of the universe roughly 14 billion years ago!

The LHC is helping scientists understand different particles, and explain more about how the universe was created.

By understanding what's happened in the past, scientists can shape the future.

Situated underground, the LHC is made up of a ring-shaped tunnel 17 miles (27 km) long!

laid end to end!

A shot in the **dark**

The universe is full of mysteries, but in 2019, very smart scientists shone new light on a spectacular **space phenomenon**.

Event Horizon Telescopes

A black hole is an area of space where a force called gravity is so strong that nothing can escape it—not even light!

Super scientists

With the combined efforts of telescope technology and brilliant brains, scientists set out to get the first image of a **black hole**. A global network of observatories called the **Event Horizon Telescope** focused about 55 million light years away from Earth. Data was collected and computer scientists created a set of instructions to produce an image.

Out of the darkness

In April 2019, an image of a black hole was displayed on screen for the first time ever. Until then, black holes **had never been seen**—scientists only knew they existed because of the impact they have on stars, dust, and galaxies around them. Thanks to scientists, we now know one more thing about the universe.

If you fell into a black hole you would be sucked inside and stretched long and thin until your body broke apart! This process is called "spaghettification."

The bright orange ring is made up of gas.

The dark spot is the shadow of the black hole.

This groundbreaking image is the first ever taken of a black hole!

Trailblazers

and **pioneers**

Most of the things people do—however amazing—have been done many times before. But, imagine doing the unthinkable and becoming the **very first** person to do something incredible. That's exactly what this groundbreaking bunch did when they dreamed big.

An unexpected
adventure

When a British ship arrived on the shores of Huahine, a small island in Polynesia, one man jumped at the chance to go on an **adventure**...

Britain

Omai

Captain Cook

I wonder what it would be like to travel on that ship.

Forming friendships

When one of British explorer Captain Cook's ships sailed to the island of Huahine, near Tahiti, a young man named **Omai** (also known as Mai) saw an opportunity. Omai was curious about Britain and befriended the crew. In 1773, Omai secured his place on board a ship headed for Britain.

Queen Charlotte

King George III

I like this fellow.

Social star

As the first Polynesian to visit Britain, everyone **wanted to meet** Omai. He was introduced to high society, posed for paintings, and had dinner with the King and Queen. He learned to ride horses, speak English, and was taught how to play backgammon and chess.

Huahine

Omai's mementos

After about two years, it was time to return home. Omai took **souvenirs** with him including a globe, umbrellas, a chess set, and a suit of armor. Back in Huahine, Omai settled down in a wooden house, complete with a garden of European plants.

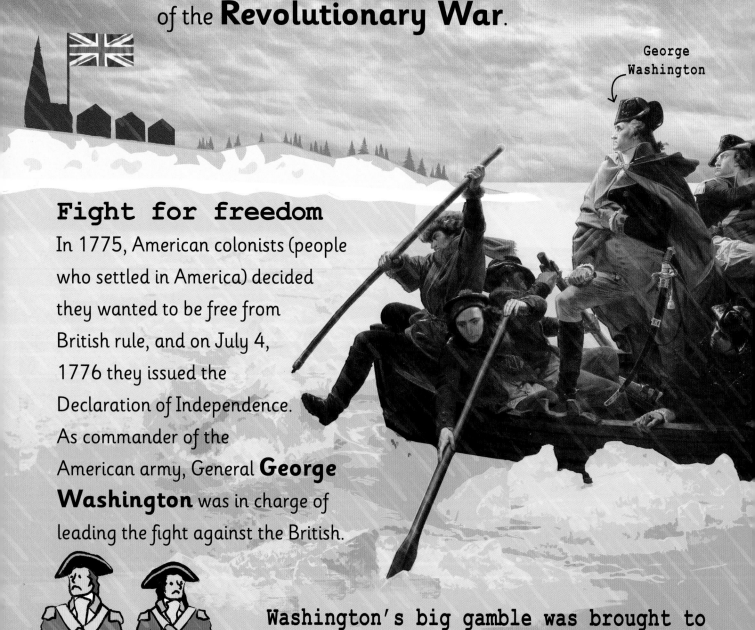

Crossing the **Delaware**

America's first president was quite the adventurer before his time in office. One of his most well-known feats was crossing the Delaware River, an event that turned the tide of the **Revolutionary War**.

George Washington

Fight for freedom

In 1775, American colonists (people who settled in America) decided they wanted to be free from British rule, and on July 4, 1776 they issued the Declaration of Independence. As commander of the American army, General **George Washington** was in charge of leading the fight against the British.

Washington's big gamble was brought to

Plan of action

By December 1776, the American army was **struggling**, and Washington badly needed a victory. He came up with a very risky plan—to cross the dangerously icy Delaware River. On Christmas evening the troops set off in small boats and spent hours battling through a harsh winter storm. Only a third managed to reach the other side.

The victory at Trenton raised the Americans' spirits and gave them hope for independence.

Surprise!

When Washington's troops reached the other side of the river, they crept up on the town of **Trenton** and launched a surprise attack. The Americans managed to win their first major victory of the revolution, and eventually, in 1783, they won the war and their independence.

George Washington became the first president of the United States in 1789.

life in a famous painting in 1851.

The fossil hunter

A lot of people enjoy searching for shells at the beach, but this woman's seaside **discoveries** transformed scientific knowledge of ancient life on Earth.

Dinosaur discovery

During the early 19th century, British schoolgirl **Mary Anning** collected seashells and fossils on her local beach. In 1811, 12-year-old Mary and her brother uncovered the complete skeleton of a large marine reptile lying beneath the sand. It turned out to be an extinct **ichthyosaur** from the **age of the dinosaurs**!

The story of Mary Anning is told in the popular children's tongue-twister, "She sells seashells by the seashore."

My brother and I sold fossils to visiting tourists.

Mary Anning

Fossils are the remains of living things that died

Unsung hero

The area became known as a hot spot for finding fossils. Although Mary had no background or training in fossil hunting, she found hundreds of fossils. At the time, paleontology—**the study of fossils**—was dominated by men, so many people didn't trust Mary's findings. Some men even took credit for her work!

Fossil ammonite

In 1823, Mary found the first complete skeleton of a long-necked swimming reptile called a plesiosaur.

Vital contributions

Mary's fossils, including ammonite, plesiosaur, and ichthyosaur skeletons, and other prehistoric creatures, enabled **scientists** to learn much more about this ancient coastline and its extinct inhabitants.

Mary Anning was a superstar!

I'm a marine reptile, not a dinosaur!

Ichthyosaur

Going for gold

A valuable precious metal, gold has an almost magical effect on people. In 1848, the lure of **finding gold** sent waves of people to California, US.

I think I've struck GOLD!

The gold rush

While James Wilson Marshall examined a riverbed, he noticed a few specks of **shiny metal**. He showed them to other people, who quickly realized he had found gold! Word spread about the gold in California, and soon, thousands of people flocked there in search of riches.

Gold

The rush for riches

Searching for gold

Fortune seekers

At first, gold mining was simple and could be done by hand. One of the most common methods was "**panning**"—running river water and sand through sifting pans to find leftover bits of gold. Eventually, machinery was needed to search for gold.

In 1849 alone, about $10 MILLION worth of gold was found. By 1852, that number jumped to $81 MILLION.

End of an era

In just a few short years, the gold rush was over. While there was still gold to be found, the amount had started to drop. But California would never be the same. To this day, millions of people who live there are **direct descendants** of those who came to seek their fortune.

San Francisco

During the gold rush, the population of nearby San Francisco jumped from about 1,000 to more than 25,000!

Road to **rescue**

This American savior risked her own life to help hundreds of people **find their freedom**.

Path to freedom

In the 1800s, many people from Africa were forced to work as slaves in the US. **The Underground Railroad** was a secret escape route to help enslaved people in the southern states head north to freedom. People called conductors helped escapees stay safe and avoid capture. One conductor was a woman and former slave named **Harriet Tubman**.

"I was conductor of the Underground Railroad for eight years, and I can say what most conductors can't say—I never ran my train off the track and I never lost a passenger."
—Harriet Tubman

Slave owners offered a reward of $40,000 for the capture of HARRIET TUBMAN.

Guiding light

Tubman was a former slave who experienced terrible hardship. After she escaped in 1849, she worked on the Underground Railroad, helping enslaved people escape from slave owners. She could have been captured, but her **bravery** and **determination** never went away.

Tubman became known as "Moses" because the biblical figure Moses also led his people to freedom.

Helping hand

Tubman never stopped helping others. When the Civil War started in 1861, she worked as a nurse and a spy to help the Union Army, which wanted to abolish slavery. She also made history as the first American woman to lead a military campaign, taking 300 troops up the Combahee River in South Carolina, to **rescue hundreds of enslaved people**.

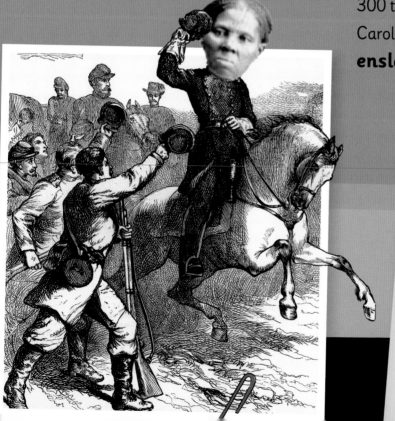

The Civil War ended in 1865 and slavery was abolished in the US. Tubman opened a home in New York where the elderly

Sailing to **freedom**

In 1862, a courageous man took an enormous risk when he **stole a boat** and sailed away from life as a slave.

Humble beginnings
Robert Smalls was born into slavery on a farm in South Carolina, US, in 1839. When he was 12, his owner sent him to the town of Charleston to work for other people. Robert got to keep a little of the money he earned, but his owner got most of it.

Trusted sailor
By 1862, Robert was working on the ships in Charleston Harbor. He was a good sailor and was trusted by the officers who commanded the ships, but they were set on keeping him enslaved.

Breaking free

Early one morning, Robert saw his opportunity to escape. He boarded a ship, taking a crew of slaves with him. They sailed to pick up their family members before sailing to **freedom**.

When they reached new waters, Robert and his crew replaced the ship's flag with a white sheet so that they wouldn't be mistaken for enemies and fired at!

Soldiers spotted the ship as it left the harbor, but Robert disguised himself as the ship's captain, so no one suspected anything.

Freedom fighter

Robert was considered a **hero** for his amazing bravery. After the war ended, he became a businessman and a politician, and spent the rest of his life fighting for the **rights** of African Americans.

Robert's former owner failed to pay taxes on his farm and therefore lost it— Robert was the one who bought it!

Daily News

USA   1887

Roaming **reporter**

This American investigative journalist went behind the scenes to expose **problems in society**, before making her own headlines by traveling around the world in record-breaking time.

Nellie Bly

HOT OFF THE PRESS

In 1885, **Nellie Bly** wrote a letter of complaint to her local paper about an article that was negative about women.

Her fiery letter impressed the paper's editor so much that he **offered her a job**.

"Energy rightly applied and directed will accomplish anything." —Nellie Bly

PRETEND PATIENT

Nellie visited slums to examine poverty and factories to investigate working conditions. She wrote about what she saw. In 1887, she faked her way into a mental institution, **undercover**, so she could experience the treatment of the patients there for herself.

After her article was published, conditions for patients improved, and Nellie became famous.

HOSPITAL HORRORS

Nellie was horrified to see filthy conditions and **rats running wild**. It was clear patients were not receiving the care they needed.

Around the World in 72 Days

Nelly raced around the world in just 72 days, setting a new record!

Record-breaking race

After reading the fictional story *Around The World in 80 Days* by the French author Jules Verne, Nellie set herself a challenge—to travel around the world in less time than the book's character! Newspaper articles chronicled her **adventures** as she traveled by boats, trains, and horses.

From East to West
and back again

The first Japanese woman to study in the US used the opportunity to further **education** for **women** in her homeland.

Japan

Girl on a mission

Born in Japan in 1864, **Tsuda Umeko**, and four other 7-year-old girls were sent to the US. Their task was to learn about Western culture. The girls were expected to come back with knowledge of how to take care of a home and raise children, but Umeko had **different ideas**.

Tsuda Umeko

Going west

Umeko spent 11 years in the US, studying everything from science and literature to art and music. She realized the knowledge she gained could **improve the lives** of women back home. When she returned to Japan, she gave speeches on the importance of women's education and the role of women in society.

US

Science
Literature
Art
Music

After studying in the US, Umeko graduated with a degree in biology.

In honor of her work, TSUDA UMEKO will be featured on the ¥5000 note starting in 2024.

Live and learn

Despite being offered the chance to stay in the US, Umeko was determined to play her part in transforming the lives of women back home. Her experiences made her an expert on education and a pioneer for change. In 1900, she founded **Tsuda College**, which remains one of the oldest women's colleges in Japan.

The fight for **rights**

Women all over the world can thank **Emmeline Pankhurst** for leading the fight for gender equality and helping women gain the right to vote.

DEEDS
NOT
WORDS

"I would rather be a rebel than a slave."
—Emmeline Pankhurst

Votes for women

Women's rights

Born in England in 1858 to a family of political activists, Emmeline was taught to stand up for what she believed in. She established the Women's Social and Political Union (WSPU) in 1903 to help get women the same **opportunities** as men, and to win women the right to vote. In 1918, women over 30 gained the right to vote, but there was more to be done.

Taking action

The WSPU did not always protest peacefully. Some women chained themselves to railings, broke windows, and started fires to highlight their cause, and many were arrested. The newspapers called them "**suffragettes**" and this is how they have been known ever since.

VOTES FOR WOMEN

In 1893, New Zealand became the first nation in which woman gained the right to vote.

WOMEN DEMAND THE VOTE

Emmeline's daughters also campaigned for the suffragettes.

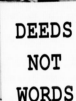

DEEDS NOT WORDS

VOTES FOR WOMEN

Votes for all

During World War I, the WSPU halted protesting so women could take on men's jobs. Imprisoned suffragettes were freed and governments looked at the WSPU in a positive light. Emmeline died in 1928, but days later, women in the UK gained the **right to vote** at 21 years old. She had won, but the journey to gender equality was not over.

Learning to **fly**

In the early 1900s, humans were on the verge of taking to the skies in the **first powered flight**. Most engineers thought powerful engines were the key, but two brothers had a different idea…

Orville Wright

Wilbur Wright

Flying machine

On a cold blustery morning in December 1903 in North Carolina, US, brothers **Orville** and **Wilbur Wright** were ready to test their invention, the Wright Flyer.

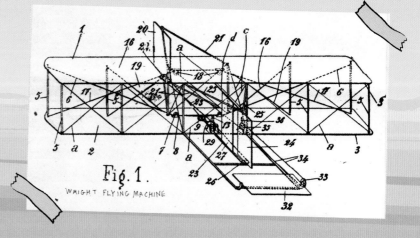

Fig. 1.

WRIGHT FLYING MACHINE

Trial and error

They had spent years testing different wing shapes, rudders, and ways of steering. They knew from working in bike manufacturing that **balance** was even more important than engine power.

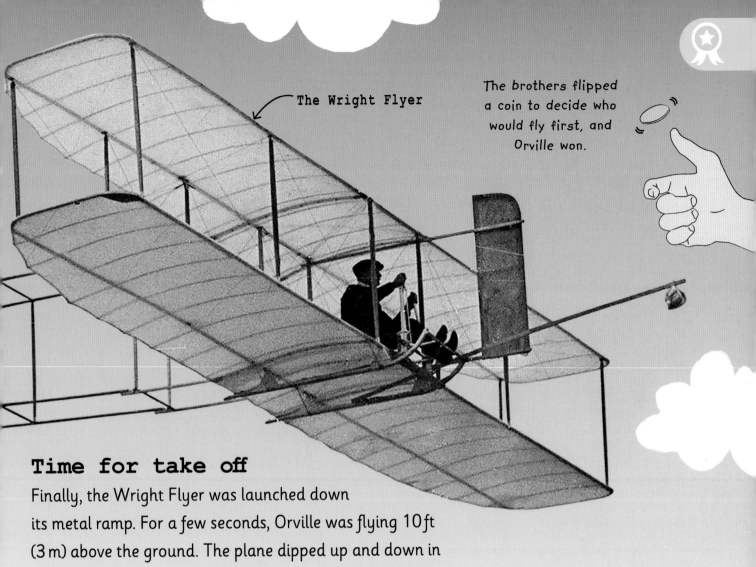

The Wright Flyer

The brothers flipped a coin to decide who would fly first, and Orville won.

Time for take off

Finally, the Wright Flyer was launched down its metal ramp. For a few seconds, Orville was flying 10 ft (3 m) above the ground. The plane dipped up and down in the air. Orville tried to control it but a strong gust of wind made it crash into the beach. But it had **worked**!

The papers weren't interested in the flight. It was only later that people realized how IMPORTANT the achievement was.

NEWS
WE'RE UNIMPRESSED BY FLIGHT

The brothers tested their plane in Kitty Hawk in North Carolina because it had steady winds and soft sand in case they crashed. Safety first!

Queen of the **skies**

In the early part of the 20th century, very few people could consider a career as a **pilot**. One incredible woman, however, defied all expectations…

Bessie Coleman

Big dreams

When she was young, **Bessie Coleman** dreamed of becoming a pilot, but no American flying schools would accept an African-American woman. Determined to find a way, Bessie saved her money, learned to speak French, and moved to France to take **flying lessons**.

Making history

In June 1921, Bessie earned her pilot's license. She soared into the history books by becoming the **first** African-American—male or female—to do so. When she returned to the US, she was considered a hero!

Bessie performed dangerous stunts for thousands of fans. With the plane in midair, she'd do figure eights, loop-the-loops, and dives.

Spectacular stunts

Despite finding fame, the only work Bessie could find was in stunt flying. It was **dangerous**, but Bessie felt she had little choice. People would gather in great crowds and pay to watch her unbelievable tricks. She became so skilled that she was soon known as **Queen Bess**, traveling the US and inspiring young girls to follow their dreams.

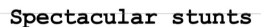

World of **wonder**

In 1922, 16 year-old Canadian-American **Idris Galcia Welsh** dreamed of adventure. When she saw an ad for a job as a female explorer, she jumped at the chance to apply. Soon, she would set off on a trip driving around the world.

Drive of a lifetime

Idris met "Cap," the leader of the **Wanderwell Expedition**, in Nice, France. She was welcomed onto his team and adopted the name **Aloha Wanderwell**. They would go on to travel through Europe, Africa, Asia, and North America, filming and taking photographs as they went.

Aloha Wanderwell

They drove under the Brandenburg Gate.

Brandenburg Gate, Germany

Between 1922 and 1927, the Wanderwell team drove through 43 COUNTRIES on 4 CONTINENTS!

Valley of the Kings, Egypt

When they reached the Great Sphinx in Egypt, the entire Wanderwell crew camped beneath it.

Taj Mahal, India

Aloha met a snake charmer in front of the Taj Mahal.

Kilauea Volcano, Hawaii

WANDERWELL WORLD TOUR

Cap filmed Aloha at the edge of Kilauea Volcano.

After falling in love on their adventure, Aloha and Cap got married in April 1925.

California, US

Aloha sometimes used crushed bananas to grease the car and keep the engine running!

Woman of many talents

After years on the road, the Wanderwells took their footage and made movies. Aloha became known as **"the world's most widely traveled girl."** A vital member of the team, she had driven and fixed the car, filmed videos, translated, made clothing, and performed stunts. She is remembered as the first woman to travel around the world by car.

Marching for **freedom**

Mahatma Gandhi

For decades, India was part of Britain's empire. **Mahatma Gandhi** was determined to end British rule, but did not believe in using violence, so he had to find other ways to make change.

Gandhi gave inspiring talks to his followers.

Marching on

For years, Indians had harvested salt from the ocean, but the British made it illegal. There was also a **high tax on salt**, making it expensive. After asking the British to remove the salt law, Gandhi received no response. So, in March 1930, he set off on foot with some followers—he had a plan to make the British listen.

Gandhi's followers called him

Making a stand

24 days later, Gandhi and his followers reached the ocean. Gandhi picked up a lump of salt—breaking the law. He was arrested, along with 60,000 other Indians. This became known as the **Salt March**.

Thousands more marchers joined Gandhi on his way to the ocean.

Freedom at last

The Salt March was the beginning of a movement. Gandhi was released from prison a year later, and continued to lead others in **peaceful protests**. In August 1947, India finally became a free country.

"MAHATMA," which means "GREAT SOUL."

Spanish
sisterhood

Clara Campoamor put women's rights at the top of the political agenda during the turbulent time of civil war.

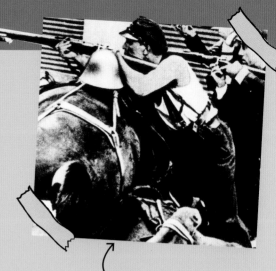

Battles in the streets of Barcelona during the Spanish Civil War.

Clara Campoamor

On a mission

Born in Madrid, Spain in 1888, Campoamor worked hard and graduated with a degree in law at a time when hardly any women went to college. She was determined to make the **world a better place** for women.

Campoamor also worked as a translator of French novels

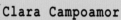

Time for change

Campoamor became deputy of the Radical Party, and led the way making the changes she wanted to see. She voiced her feelings that people should not be treated differently because of their gender, so **women should have the same voting rights as men**. She gave many inspirational speeches, and eventually, the Spanish courts passed new laws to give women in Spain the vote.

Lasting legacy

Campoamor moved to Argentina and then Switzerland, where she put pen to paper to write about her life's work. She had changed the course of **women's rights** in Spain, giving women greater freedom and more opportunities. In the face of protests, she stood up for women's rights until history was made.

and wrote BIOGRAPHIES of other people's lives.

Pioneering **pilot**

Amelia Earhart made history as the first woman to fly a plane solo across the Atlantic Ocean, earning her headlines around the world.

A head for heights

Amelia grew up in America and was a **daredevil** starting at an early age. She once built a ramp on the roof of her family's shed and "flew" down the ramp in a wooden box. Although she got hurt, she loved the experience.

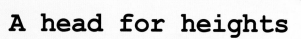

AVIATION CLUB

As Amelia grew, so did her interest in flying. Not many women were involved in aviation at that time. But that didn't stop her.

Amelia was the president of an aviation club for women and wrote many articles about flying.

In January of 1935, Amelia broke another record

Making history

In 1927, pilot Charles Lindbergh made history when he flew a plane across the Atlantic Ocean. A year later, Amelia successfully made the same journey with two other pilots. She was thrilled but hoped for the chance to make the same flight again—but this time **by herself**.

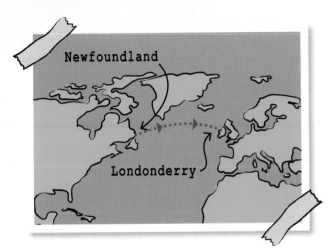

Newfoundland

Londonderry

Moment of truth

That chance came in 1932. After taking off from Newfoundland, Canada, Amelia battled mechanical problems and a severe thunderstorm. She was forced to make an unexpected landing near Londonderry, Northern Ireland, but she had **achieved her dream**—she'd flown solo across the Atlantic Ocean!

Amelia landed in a field where she was spotted by farmers. It was so unusual for a woman to pilot a plane, they assumed she was a boy!

when she flew SOLO from CALIFORNIA to HAWAII.

Animal antics

This committed conservationist turned her **time with chimpanzees** into the longest ever continuous study of an animal in its natural habitat.

"If we do not do something to help these creatures, we make a mockery of the whole concept of justice."
—Jane Goodall

Wild at heart

Although **Jane Goodall** was born in bustling London in 1934, she wanted to be in the wild. At 26, she visited Gombe National Park in Tanzania, Africa, to **study chimpanzees**. This marked the beginning of more than 50 years of scientific study.

Gombe National Park

Tanzania

Making connections

In time, the wild chimps grew to recognize and accept Jane. She noticed they had **different personalities** and emotions, just like people. She observed them taking care of friends and fighting with enemies, and marveled at their ability to make **tools** from rocks and sticks.

A chimpanzee using a stem to soak up water.

Chimp conservation

In 1977, Jane set up the Jane Goodall Institute. To this day, the organization continues to research and protect chimps **in the wild**. Jane has published many books about her work, and won many wildlife and conservation awards.

Reach for the stars

In 1963, **Valentina Tereshkova** wrote her own extraordinary chapter in the story of space exploration when she became the first woman to enter space.

Space cadet

Valentina was born in Russia in 1937. Her favorite hobby was parachute jumping, which helped her get chosen for the **Russian space program**. She beat out more than 400 other applicants before she was finally selected to go into space.

"Once you've been in space, you appreciate...

Secret space mission

Valentina endured six months of intensive training in preparation for space, including experiencing weightlessness and isolation. She pretended to her parents that she was taking part in a parachute competition!

Valentina's voyage

On June 16, 1963, Valentina was launched on a solo mission into space on board spacecraft Vostok 6. She became the **first woman** in space, making 48 orbits of Earth over nearly three days.

how small and fragile the Earth is." –Valentina Tereshkova

Valentina married Russian cosmonaut Andrian Nikolayev. Their daughter, Elena, became the first child born to parents who had both been to space!

National treasure

Valentina was awarded the title **Hero of the Soviet Union** (Russia) for her achievement. She never returned to space, but she paved the way for other women to become astronauts.

Rowing into the record books

John claims he saw UFOs on his journey!

In the same year humans first walked on the moon, this British rower made a splash by becoming the first person to row **solo across** an ocean.

Boy Scout turned seafarer

As a young boy **John Fairfax** read adventure stories and learned survival skills in the Boy Scouts. After reading about two Norwegians who **rowed across the Atlantic Ocean**, Fairfax vowed to go one better and do it alone.

On my journey I made friends with a dolphin I named "Jerrycan."

Britannia

BRITANNIA

Going solo

In 1969, Fairfax set off from the **Canary Islands**, off the coast of Africa, in a boat named Britannia with only himself for company. He had to overcome raging storms, circling sharks, and survive on limited supplies and the occasional fish he could catch. After rowing for more than **180 days**, he arrived in Florida, US.

Atlantic Ocean

John Fairfax

Sylvia Cook

Pacific pair

Two years later, Fairfax and his girlfriend Sylvia Cook set off to row across the **Pacific**, the world's biggest ocean. The Pacific is a lot bigger than the Atlantic, but after **363 days** they completed their goal and earned their place in the record books.

Pacific Ocean

The couple's Pacific adventure had its share of troubles. Fairfax was bitten by a shark and they got caught in a cyclone!

The lone **adventurer**

Most explorers and thrill seekers travel with others. This adventurer, however, made his name by performing feats that were usually done as a team, **by himself**.

Early adventures

Naomi Uemura was born in Japan in 1941. As a boy, he was shy and lacked confidence in himself. To overcome this, he took part in athletic activities, and fell in love with hiking in the wilderness and climbing mountains.

Uemura led an amazing life filled with adventure.

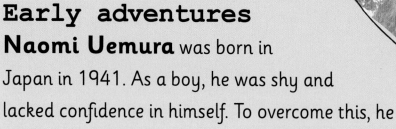

He rafted the length of the **Amazon River** over two months.

He walked the **full length** of Japan in 53 days.

Flying solo

Uemura spent years challenging himself by going on difficult expeditions alone. After years of adventuring, he embarked on one of his biggest challenges yet—a solo climb of **Denali**, North America's tallest mountain, in the winter.

Disappearance

During the climb, Uemura made it to the peak of Denali, but on the way down he disappeared without a trace. A rescue party found some gear and his diary, but sadly he was never seen again. Naomi is remembered as a **great hero** in Japan and by adventurers everywhere.

These are just a few of his incredible solo feats:

He climbed **Mount Kilimanjaro**, the tallest peak in Africa.

He became the **first person** to reach the North Pole solo. He got there by dogsled in 54 days.

Born to be **wild**

When it came to **protecting** the world's wildlife, this croc-catching conservationist had a big personality and a heart to match.

Irwin caught his first venomous snake when he was six years old.

Croc catcher

Australian **Steve Irwin** was born in 1962 and grew up surrounded by animals. His parents protected wild reptiles and his father took him into the Australian outback to catch crocodiles, snakes, and lizards. As a young man, Irwin would rescue crocodiles before hunters could shoot them.

Stingray

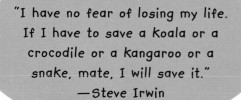

"I have no fear of losing my life. If I have to save a koala or a crocodile or a kangaroo or a snake, mate, I will save it."
—Steve Irwin

Famous face

TV producers saw video footage of Irwin in action and gave him his own show, *The Crocodile Hunter*, in 1992. Viewers loved his **tremendous courage** and excitable character. Irwin was watched by 500 million people in more than 100 countries.

Irwin confessed he was scared of parrots because they had bitten him *so* many times!

Continuing conservation

Irwin worked with animals that were **dangerous** and often **endangered**. In 2006, he was tragically killed by a stingray, but his wife, Terri, and two children, Robert and Bindi, continue his conservation efforts.

"Survival can be summed up in three words—never give up. That's the heart of it really. Just keep trying."
—Bear Grylls

Born survivor

What would you take to a desert island? Forget a good book, a comfy pillow, or a bottle of water… all you really need is **Bear Grylls**!

On top of the world

British adventurer Bear Grylls was born in 1974. He loved the outdoors, where his father taught him to climb, hike, and sail. As an adult, he joined the Special Air Service (SAS) in the British Army and honed his **survival skills**. After a parachuting accident that broke his back, Grylls recovered and climbed Mount Everest at 23.

Thrills and spills

After Mount Everest, Grylls sought new adventures. He traveled across the Atlantic Ocean in a tiny boat, and tried powered paragliding over Angel Falls in Venezuela. He even got the **world record** for the highest formal meal, when he ate a three course dinner in a hot air balloon, before skydiving back down to Earth!

Grylls was a Cub Scout as a boy, and was made Chief Scout in 2009.

Survival tactics

Extreme conditions have taken their toll on Grylls. He once kept cool in the scorching desert sun by peeing on his shirt and wearing it on his head! He has also resorted to eating giant larva worms, yak eyeballs, and deer poop. Yuck!

Yak eyeballs

Deer poop

Giant lava worms

Gryll's television programs have been watched by more than TWO BILLION PEOPLE around the world.

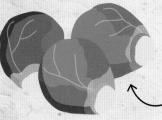

Although Grylls has eaten some terrible things, the thing he hates most is brussels sprouts!

Making **waves**

Laura Dekker followed her dreams and battled the high seas in her quest to become the youngest person to sail solo around the world.

Laura Dekker

Setting sail

Laura started sailing solo at 6 years old. At 13, she set her heart on **sailing around the world**. The Dutch authorities said she was too young to make the journey alone. Laura appealed, and in 2010, at 14, she set sail from the Caribbean aboard her boat, *Guppy*.

Laura's highlights included encounters

Trouble at sea

There were many **challenges** along the way: *Guppy's* sails got stuck, and Laura almost crashed into a container ship. She experienced stormy weather and giant waves. Her only traveling companions were cockroaches and ants crawling on the deck!

Land ho!

After 518 days, Laura, now 16, delighted waiting crowds when she returned to the Caribbean as the **youngest** person to sail around the world solo!

Guppy

Laura wrote a blog of her adventures and even kept up to date with homework on her journey!

with PENGUINS, DOLPHINS, and WHALES!

Builders, creators,

and **thinkers**

You don't have to climb a mountain or travel into outer space to be an adventurer. Some of the most extraordinary boundaries have been broken by people who simply dared to **think big**, rip up the rule book, and follow their own path...

The story of **silk**

Ancient China's best-kept secret was the creation of a **luxurious thread** used to make clothes for rulers and royalty.

Smooth as silk

Silk comes from **silkworm moths**. These creatures start life as caterpillars that spin silk to create protective **cocoons** as they become moths. This silk can be turned into a very soft fabric.

Silkworm moth

Silk gown

Caterpillar

Cocoons

Top secret

Legend has it that **Empress Leizu** of ancient China spotted shiny threads made by silkworms in her mulberry tree. As a result, she invented the **loom** to produce silk, and a new industry was born. Silk, however, was kept secret in China for about a thousand years.

At the time, anyone who shared information about silk or took silkworms outside China was punished.

Around the year 500 CE, the story goes that the Roman emperor Justinian paid monks to smuggle silkworm eggs out of China, so his empire could reap the rewards. Silk was secret no more.

Traders traveled thousands of miles along the Silk Road to get this expensive fabric.

The Silk Road

Rulers around the world wanted to get their hands on silk, but for a long time China was the **only source**. Silk was crafted and transported along a **trade route**, which became known as the Silk Road because of it.

Silk is still a popular luxury fabric today.

The wise and fair
philosopher

Over 2,500 years ago, a Chinese man named **Confucius** came up with some big ideas that would have a long-lasting impact on the world.

Treat others kindly

Forging his own path

Confucius was born in 551 BCE into a powerful family. He began working in government, but after voicing his ideas about what was right and wrong, he made some enemies. Confucius decided to leave his job and become a **teacher**.

Confucius's philosophy includes:

Respect your elders

Have good manners

Be fair and ethical

Don't be greedy

Obey the government

Fair and just

After opening a school in his hometown, Confucius soon taught thousands of students. Unlike most schools at the time, his was open to **everyone**—both rich and poor. He developed and taught his own philosophy, which were rules about the right way to live.

A wise man

Confucius's teachings were based on **truth**, **justice**, and good **social relations**. Although his writing was not popular right away, the ideas later became adopted by future Chinese emperors, providing guidelines for how to rule and lead by example.

Confucius's teachings and sayings are recorded in a book called *The Analects*, which is still popular today.

Confucian temple

A monument through time

Hagia Sophia was built as a cathedral in Constantinople (now Istanbul, Turkey) between 532 and 537. Since then, it has undergone many changes…

"This should be a monument for all

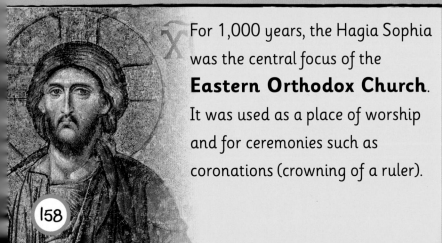

For 1,000 years, the Hagia Sophia was the central focus of the **Eastern Orthodox Church**. It was used as a place of worship and for ceremonies such as coronations (crowning of a ruler).

In 1453, Sultan Mehmed II conquered Constantinople and changed Hagia Sophia from a church to an **Islamic mosque**. The altar and bells were removed, and Christian-themed mosaic tiles were covered.

Hagia Sophia is 1,400 YEARS OLD.

A story of change
This iconic building shows the changes in society over hundreds of years. It began as a cathedral, was turned into a mosque, and is now a museum.

In 1934, the Turkish Republic's first president, Kemal Atatürk, stopped Hagia Sophia from being used as a religious meeting place.

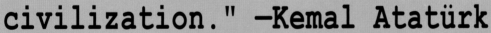

civilization." –Kemal Atatürk

After nearly 500 years as a mosque, Hagia Sophia was made into a museum and has been one ever since. The museum reflects the **diverse history** of the building, combining elements of Christian and Islamic art and decoration.

Kemal Atatürk

Measuring the **Earth**

Have you ever wondered how big the Earth is? Or how you might find out? Over 2,000 years ago, a very smart **mathematician** decided to do just that.

Sun

Eratosthenes

Reflecting rays

One day in Syene, Egypt, the Greek mathematician **Eratosthenes** noticed that when he looked down a well, the sun's rays reflected off the water and bounced straight back out. He realized this meant the sun was directly above him, but he also realized it only happened **once a year**, on the summer solstice (the longest day of the year).

Curious angles

One year later, on the summer solstice in Alexandria, 500 miles (800 km) from Syene, Eratosthenes observed that the sun's rays didn't fall directly down—they fell at a **slight angle**. He used the height of a pillar and the length of its shadow to figure out that the angle was 7.2°

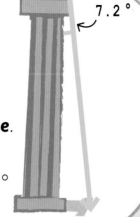

7.2°

Tricky calculations

Earth is a circle, and circles are made up of 360°. Eratosthenes figured out that 7.2 goes into 360 50 times. So he multiplied 50 by the distance between Syene and Alexandria, which is 500 miles (800 km) and got **25,000**.

Alexandria

Syene

We now know the distance around Earth is about 24,901 miles (40,075 km). Eratosthenes was very close!

Eratosthenes was the first person to accurately estimate the size of Earth. What's even more amazing is that at the time many people believed the world was flat!

Center of Earth

Hidden city

The chance discovery of a mysterious city in the mountains of Peru revealed one of the world's **best-kept secrets.**

Hidden gem

For centuries, a city had remained hidden amid the swirling clouds of the Andes Mountains. American historian **Hiram Bingham** was tipped off by a local farmer that ancient ruins were located among the lofty peaks. In 1911, he found **Machu Picchu**, the ruins of an Inca settlement.

Hiram Bingham

Machu Picchu has more than 150 buildings and 100 staircases!

MACHU PICCHU was voted one of the New SEVEN WONDERS OF THE WORLD in 2007.

An ancient empire

The Inca Empire was based in Peru, but spread down the west coast of South America. Starting as a small tribe of American Indian people in the 1400s, it eventually became home to more than 10 million people. After suffering civil war and disease, the empire ended when Spanish conqueror Francisco Pizarro arrived in 1532 to seize riches.

I took a few souvenirs home.

Inca Empire

Francisco Pizarro

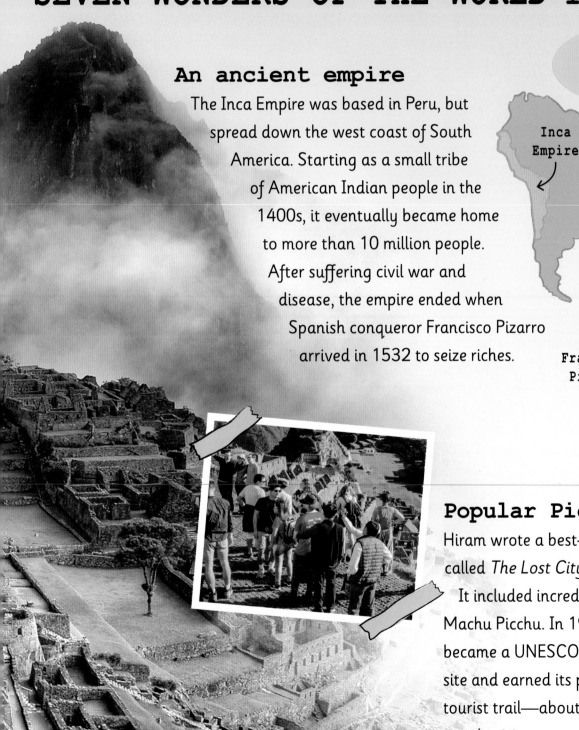

Popular Picchu

Hiram wrote a best-selling book called *The Lost City of the Incas*. It included incredible details of Machu Picchu. In 1983, Machu Picchu became a UNESCO World Heritage site and earned its place on the tourist trail—about 1,000,000 people visit every year!

163

Despite what many people think, Michelangelo painted standing up—not lying on his back. It caused him a lot of discomfort and pain!

Michelangelo painted 343 people onto the ceiling.

The section of the ceiling called "The Creation of Adam" is one of the most famous pieces of art in the world.

Backbreaking work

Michelangelo spent **four years** painting the 65 ft (20 m) high ceiling while standing on scaffolding. It was worth the effort—it has become one of the most famous and impressive works of art in history, and as many as 25,000 people visit it every day!

Michelangelo's masterpiece

The ceiling of the Sistine Chapel in Rome is an **artistic wonder**. It took one incredible man four years of painstaking work to complete it.

Magnificent Michelangelo

Michelangelo was an Italian painter, sculptor, architect, and poet, born in 1475. He dedicated his whole life to **art**, creating masterpieces for many rich and powerful people.

The reluctant artist

The pope wanted Michelangelo to paint a magnificent scene for the **ceiling** of the Sistine Chapel in Rome. Michelangelo didn't want to accept the job at first because he preferred sculpting to painting. But in 1508 he agreed, and work began.

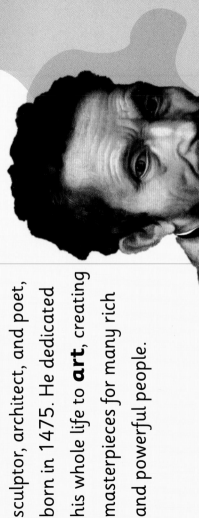

Musical
marvel

This genius composer created some of the best music of all time—despite losing his **sense of hearing**.

"Music comes to me more readily than words."
—Ludwig Van Beethoven

Gifted musician

Ludwig van Beethoven was born in Germany in 1770. He came from a musical family and became an excellent pianist. Beethoven didn't enjoy school, and at the age of 10, he quit to study music.

Making music

Before he was 30, Beethoven had written many successful pieces of music and was already one of the most famous and important musicians in the world. But something was wrong—he began to hear **buzzing** in his ears.

Beethoven wowed audiences with his amazing compositions, such as The Moonlight Sonata.

Secret struggle

Beethoven was secretly losing his hearing. By the time he was 46, he was **completely deaf**. But he didn't give up. The depth of his musical knowledge meant he could still compose amazing music from memory without needing to hear it.

When his hearing troubles began, Beethoven used a special hearing trumpet.

One theory of how Beethoven lost his hearing was that he used to dip his head in cold water to stay awake, but nobody knows for sure.

167

Story time

In the early 1800s, two brothers changed the face of storytelling by producing the world's first collection of **fairy tales**.

Once upon a time

For centuries, people have enjoyed sharing folk tales. Traditionally, these stories were spoken, not written down. German brothers, Jacob and Wilhelm Grimm, gathered these stories together in a **collection** for adults to study.

Classic stories

Later, the Grimm brothers changed the folk tales to make them more appealing to children. In 1812, their first volume of 86 stories was published, including *Snow White*, *Hansel and Gretel*, *Rapunzel*, *Rumpelstiltskin*, and *Little Red Riding Hood*. The collection has become known as **Grimm's Fairy Tales** and many of its stories are still read by children all over the world!

By 1857, *Grimm's Fairy Tales* had expanded from 86 to 211 stories!

Grimm's Fairy Tales

Wilhelm Grimm

Jacob Grimm

A color illustration of *Sleeping Beauty* was used in an 1865 version of *Grimm's Fairy Tales*.

The Grimm brothers paved the way for more fairy tales from other countries. In 1835, *Fairy Tales Told for Children.* by Danish storyteller Hans Christian Andersen was published.

Hans Christian Andersen

Mary Shelley

The story behind a
scary story

Volcanic eruptions are known for creating heat, but Mount Tambora's eruption was famous for the chill it caused. Amazingly, it may have also led to the creation of one of the most **famous books** ever.

In 1815, Mount Tambora in Indonesia erupted. The ash from the volcano blocked out the sun and made the planet colder. The effects were so dramatic that the following year became known as **the year without a summer**.

During that summer, writer **Mary Shelley** and her friends were on a trip to Lake Geneva in Switzerland. The weather was so bad that they were stuck indoors and became very bored.

To pass the time, they held a competition to see who could come up with the best **scary story**. Inspired by a dream and the storm outside, Mary wrote about a mad scientist who created a monster and brought it to life using **lightning**.

Mary called her story "FRANKENSTEIN."

Frankenstein became one of the most famous and important books ever written. We'll never know if it would exist if Mount Tambora hadn't erupted!

Frankenstein

Inspiring others

Being blind and deaf did not stop **Helen Keller** from becoming one of the most inspirational women in history.

Top teacher

Helen was born in the US in 1880. At only 19 months old, she came down with an illness which left her deaf and blind for the rest of her life. She learned to communicate by creating her own **sign language**, and practiced finger spelling with her teacher, **Anne Sullivan**.

Anne Sullivan

Helen Keller

Anne ran water over Helen's hand, then spelled w-a-t-e-r on her fingers.

Lifelong partners

Helen and Anne worked together for 49 years! Helen learned to talk by feeling Anne's face and the vibrations she made when she spoke. Soon, Helen was **giving speeches** and helping other people who were deaf or blind during her travels to 35 countries around the world.

Alexander Graham Bell, the inventor of the telephone, helped teach deaf children and was friends with Helen.

Helen learned to read braille, which uses raised dots to represent letters. Braille is still used by blind people today.

Braille

Bridging the gap

The **Brooklyn Bridge** in New York, US, was only half finished when Washington Roebling, the chief engineer, got sick. Who would finish the job?

Before Emily

John Roebling

Washington Augustus Roebling

Washington was not the first chief engineer to hand over the project. His father's foot was crushed and he died from complications. It was very lucky that Emily knew her husband's work well, and was smart, skilled, and determined.

Emily to the rescue

Help came from an unexpected place—Washington's wife **Emily Roebling**. Emily was not a trained engineer, and in the late 1800s, it was highly unusual for a woman to work in construction. Some people didn't believe she could do the job.

It took 14 years for the Brooklyn Bridge to be built.

Success

Building the bridge was difficult and demanding work.
However, on May 24, 1883, it was officially finished.
President Chester Arthur opened the bridge, and
Emily was the first person to cross it.
This **national hero** had not
only helped complete the bridge,
but paved the way toward
gender equality.

Emily
Roebling

New York's Brooklyn Bridge
is considered one of the
greatest engineering feats
of the modern age.

The gift of liberty

What is the biggest present you can think of? Is it as big as the **Statue of Liberty**? Because in 1886, France gave this supersized statue to the US as a gift!

Gustave Eiffel

Frédéric-Auguste Bartholdi

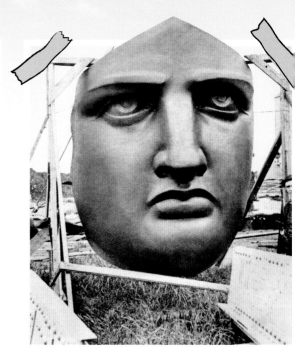

Lady Liberty

The Statue of Liberty was a gift from France to celebrate its friendship with the US. The sculptor **Frédéric-Auguste Bartholdi** got busy with the design, while the creator of the Eiffel Tower, **Gustave Eiffel**, constructed the statue's frame.

A giant gesture

The statue was built in France, and **shipped across the ocean** in lots of smaller pieces. In 1886, it was assembled on Liberty Island in New York Harbor. Standing 305 ft (93 m) tall, the Statue of Liberty was the world's tallest iron structure at the time.

Lady Liberty's torch lights the way to freedom.

Today, Liberty Island is a popular tourist spot that people can visit by ferry.

The statue is based on Libertas, the Roman goddess of freedom.

Originally shiny brown, the statue is now green. The color developed over time as chemical reactions changed the statue's copper covering.

Facing southeast, the statue is a welcoming symbol for ships entering New York Harbor.

The Statue of Liberty was the first thing that millions of immigrants saw when they reached America.

Adventure
stories

French writer **Jules Verne** put pen to paper and sparked the imaginations of millions of readers, transporting them to the bottom of the ocean and beyond...

Jules Verne

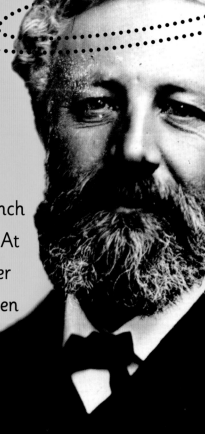

Inspirational stories

Born in 1828, Jules grew up around **adventure**. He lived in Nantes—a French port full of ships going to amazing places. At school, his teacher would tell him about her husband, a sailor who she thought had been shipwrecked and who she hoped would return one day.

Adventure writing

In 1863, after writing plays, Jules was asked to write an exciting and educational story for a travel magazine. He wrote a story called *Five Weeks in a Balloon* about three men exploring Africa. This was the first book in a series he called *Extraordinary Voyages*.

Jules spent hours in the library researching and learning about the world.

Escaping reality

The books Jules wrote were very popular. People enjoyed how he helped readers imagine places they had never been. His most popular story was called *Around the World in 80 Days*, about a man who traveled the globe.

Yuri Gagarin

Lasting legacy

Jules's stories are still popular today and have been made into many plays and movies. Famous explorers, such as cosmonaut Yuri Gagarin, said that Jules **inspired** their own adventures.

179

Exploring
West Africa

British explorer **Mary Kingsley** loved to study people, culture, and animals. In 1893, she packed up her things and made a solo journey to the unfamiliar lands of West Africa.

Journey into the unknown

At the time, Britain ruled several African countries, but no one in Britain really knew much about the people living there. They mistakenly thought Africa was full of disease and strange people. West Africa was known as "**the deadliest place on Earth**" but Mary ignored this and traveled there anyway.

Mary often traveled by canoe. She journeyed along rivers so that she could visit more places and study fish, which she was especially interested in.

Mary Kingsley met the King of Calabar, Nigeria, on her first expedition.

Independent woman

Hardly anyone from Europe had lived with Africans, and female explorers were even more rare, but Mary was **not put off by** her critics. She visited tribes, lived among locals, and learned all about their culture. She also looked for new animals.

Mary insisted on wearing blouses, full skirts, and dresses—just as she would have worn in Britain.

Truth teller

Mary traveled to Africa twice, and published two best-selling books about her findings. She proved to Europeans that Africa was not a scary place, and that Africans were **just like them**—people with an amazing culture that should be left untouched.

The unfinished
masterpiece

In 1882, work began on the magnificent **Sagrada Família** in Barcelona, Spain. But building of the church is not due be completed until 2026!

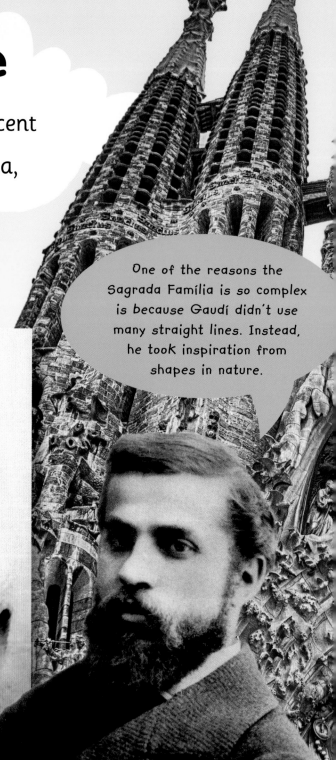

One of the reasons the Sagrada Família is so complex is because Gaudí didn't use many straight lines. Instead, he took inspiration from shapes in nature.

Ambitious architect

Antoni Gaudí was the architect behind the Sagrada Família. He spent more than 40 years perfecting his **complex designs** for the building. But the plans were so grand, it was clear he wouldn't live to see his finished masterpiece.

The Sagrada Família will likely take 144 years to build.

Obstacles

The world has changed a lot since building work began on the Sagrada Família. War, disease, protests, and a shortage of money have all delayed construction. During the Spanish Civil War in 1936, Gaudí's plans for the church were even destroyed in a fire. But despite these setbacks, new architects have stepped in to **continue Gaudí's work**.

Not long now

The entrance fee from its **4.5 million visitors** every year, as well as public donations, will soon make Gaudí's ambitious plans a reality. The beautiful building is due to be finished by 2026—exactly 100 years after Gaudí's death.

The Great Pyramid only took 20!

Undersea explorer

Born in France in 1910, **Jacques Cousteau** became passionate about undersea exploration. Much of our underwater world was a complete mystery until he came along.

Aqua-Lung

Jacques Cousteau

Deep-sea dreaming

In the early 1900s, there wasn't much technology that allowed people to **explore seas and oceans**. So, in 1943, Jacques Cousteau and a friend, engineer Émile Gagnan, developed a device that allowed divers to breathe underwater. It was a tank filled with compressed air, and they called it the **Aqua-Lung**.

Jacques believed people could live and work at sea. In 1962, his team built the first underwater habitat, and two people lived there for a week!

Jacques helped create the first underwater vehicle for ocean exploration. It's known as the "diving saucer."

Ocean exploration

Jacques did a lot of **scientific research**, mostly aboard his famous ship *Calypso*. In 1996, it was rammed by a barge and sank! It had to be brought up and towed away for repairs.

Diving saucer

Awash with talent

Jacques shared his love of the seas and oceans with the world. He made movies, wrote books, and took photos. Many of his television documentaries became hugely popular, inspiring millions of people to **take care of** Earth's underwater habitats.

No place like home

This best-selling poet and author left rural life behind to **travel** abroad, before finding that home is where the heart is.

Laurie Lee

Home sweet home

Known as "Laurie" since his birth in 1914, **Laurence Lee** grew up in a rural English village with his mother and six siblings. His childhood was spent roaming free in the woods that surrounded their home.

"Before I left the valley I thought everywhere was like this. Then I went away for 40 years and when I came back I realised that nowhere was like this."
—Laurie Lee

Leaving the nest

One morning in 1934, Lee left his country home and walked to London. But he soon grew restless and wanted to **see more of the world**. He boarded a boat to Spain where he explored on foot for four years, scraping together a living by playing the violin. Lee enjoyed the experience but missed home.

The wanderer returns

When the Spanish Civil War started, Lee helped fight for freedom in Spain, but wherever he went, he was always drawn back to his **childhood home**. In the 1960s, he returned home and wrote books and poetry for the remainder of his life.

Pioneer of **pop**

The American poster boy for popular culture created **masterpieces** for the masses.

"Everyone will be famous for 15 minutes."
—Andy Warhol

Trailblazing artist Andy Warhol grew up in the US during the 1930s. He studied art and developed a love of different media, including painting and photography. His art was displayed in galleries, but he wanted to shake up traditions and give the world a **new style of art**.

Andy Warhol

Warhol wanted his work to be both appealing and affordable.

Fame and fortune

By the 1960s, Warhol had set up a studio called "The Factory" in New York where many creative people gathered. He was part of a new **pop art** movement, which broke the traditions of fine art by featuring ordinary products and celebrities. Warhol became the movement's most famous face.

Warhol repeated products and faces in his work.

Warhol's art featured images of common goods, like soup cans.

Art for all

Today, Warhol's art is instantly recognizable. His images captured movie stars and music legends multiple times, but with a variety of **bold** colors and photographic effects added. The simple printing techniques he used to make them meant anyone could own a work by Warhol. The pop art movement is still popular and continues today.

By silk-screening images onto canvas, Warhol could quickly reproduce a piece of art many times.

Man vs. **machine**

When one of the world's best board-game players pitted his powerful brain against the most advanced artificial intelligence, who would come out **on top?**

> "There is an entity that cannot be defeated, Artificial Intelligence."
> —Lee Sedol

Give it a try

Lee Sedol was born in South Korea in 1983 and began playing the game **Go** as a child. Sedol grew up to become a professional Go player with 18 world championship titles and a huge fan base who admired his creativity and skill.

The prize for the winner was $1 MILLION.

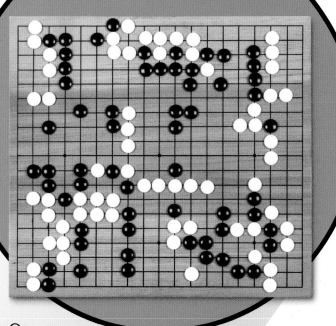

Go is an ancient game from China where players use strategy and creative thinking to gain pieces and dominate a board.

Going gets tough

The technology company Google developed an AI **(artificial intelligence)** computer program known as "AlphaGo," and wanted to test its ability by facing the best Go players. After AlphaGo beat the European champion, it was time to face the master, Sedol. Sedol confidently claimed he would win in a landslide, but the pressure was on…

Worthy winner

Sedol put forth a great effort, but AlphaGo was too strong. The program has played itself countless times, is **always learning**, and unlike Sedol, never needs to rest. Sedol lost the first three games, but managed to win the fourth, and lost 4-1 overall.

Lee Sedol's nickname is "The Strong Stone."

Although Sedol lost, it's an incredible achievement to win a game against such a powerful machine.

After the match it was donated to **CHARITY.**

The gift of **giving**

This **billionaire couple** use their big hearts and big fortune to make the **world a better place**.

Computer genius

American **Bill Gates** made his fortune from a love of computers. In 1974, Gates and his friend **Paul Allen** set up their own software company and called it **Microsoft**. Microsoft became one of the biggest companies in the world, making Gates and Allen very rich.

The Gates Foundation's key belief is that all lives have equal value.

Bill Gates has personally donated more than $36 billion to the charity.

Giving back

Gates wanted to use his money to help people, so he and his wife, Melinda, set up the **Bill and Melinda Gates Foundation** in 2000. This foundation funds projects to improve the lives of people all over the world. It works to promote equality for everyone—whether rich or poor—and focuses on **health**, **education**, and **climate change**.

Making change

The foundation has helped communities in developing countries, and donated billions toward the fight to wipe out diseases such as **malaria** and **polio**.

Bill Gates

Melinda Gates

In 2016, Bill and Melinda were awarded the Presidential Medal of Freedom for their generosity.

Daredevils and

risk takers

It's normally human nature to avoid taking big risks, but some brave (or bananas!) thrill seekers laugh in the face of danger, and attempt unbelievable **feats** that leave spectators quaking in their boots! Strap yourself in for some hair-raising stunts and terrifying tricks.

A breathtaking
balloonist

In the early 19th century, balloonists put on amazing aerial shows. **Sophie Blanchard** was the world's first professional female balloonist, and one of the most popular.

Show in the sky

Sophie was born in France, but her amazing balloon shows made her famous all over Europe. When she was in the air, she would launch **fireworks** from her balloon and lower dogs on parachutes down to the amazed crowds below.

Napoléon Bonaparte

Popular performer

Sophie performed for many important people, including the emperor of France, **Napoléon Bonaparte**. He was so impressed by Sophie he named her the "Aeronaut of the Official Festivals" and asked her to perform at his special occasions.

Surprisingly, Sophie claimed she scared easily and was frightened of loud noises. In the air, however, she was fearless.

End of an era

Ballooning was dangerous. In 1819, tragedy struck. While performing, one of Sophie's fireworks made her **balloon catch fire** and crash. Sophie is remembered as one of **history's great flyers**.

Not all people understood how balloons flew. On one trip, Sophie landed in a field and was chased away by locals with sticks who thought she was a flying demon!

America's first
daredevil

What's the scariest thing you've ever done? It probably doesn't hold a candle to the daring feats of Sam Patch, the **Jersey Jumper**!

> "Napoleon was a great man and a great general. He conquered armies and he conquered nations, but he couldn't jump the Genesee Falls."
> —Sam Patch

Sam Patch

Jump start

Born in the US in 1807, **Sam Patch** lived his short life to the fullest. As a boy, he showed off to his friends by jumping from a local bridge into the river. As he got older, he was prepared to risk his life performing jumps before a paying audience.

High Falls

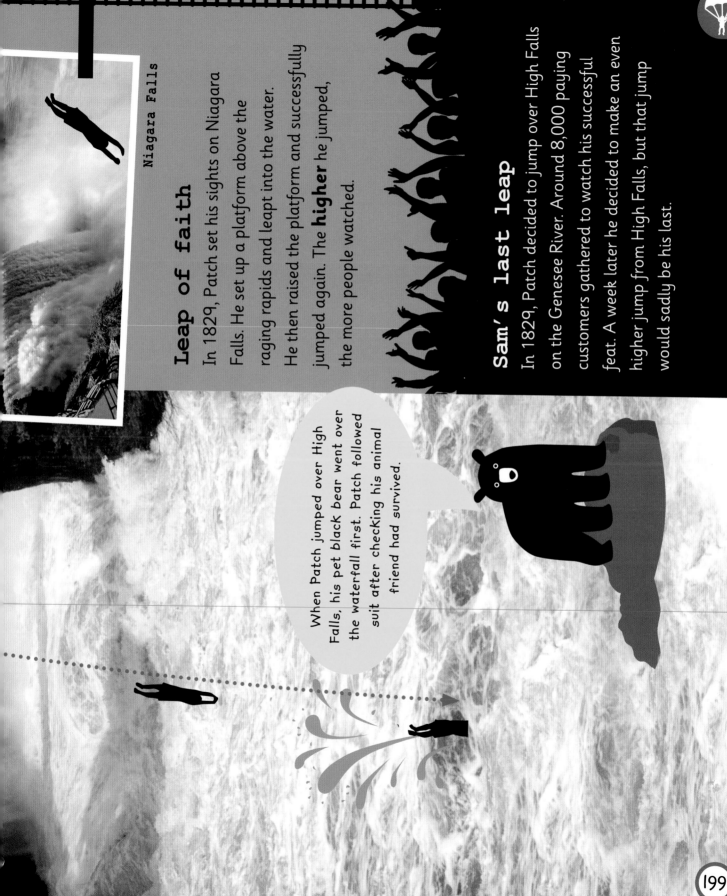

Niagara Falls

Leap of faith

In 1829, Patch set his sights on Niagara Falls. He set up a platform above the raging rapids and leapt into the water. He then raised the platform and successfully jumped again. The **higher** he jumped, the more people watched.

Sam's last leap

In 1829, Patch decided to jump over High Falls on the Genesee River. Around 8,000 paying customers gathered to watch his successful feat. A week later he decided to make an even higher jump from High Falls, but that jump would sadly be his last.

When Patch jumped over High Falls, his pet black bear went over the waterfall first. Patch followed suit after checking his animal friend had survived.

Balancing act

Most visitors to Niagara Falls are happy to take photos and enjoy the view. But **Charles Blondin** crossed the great waterfall on a tightrope!

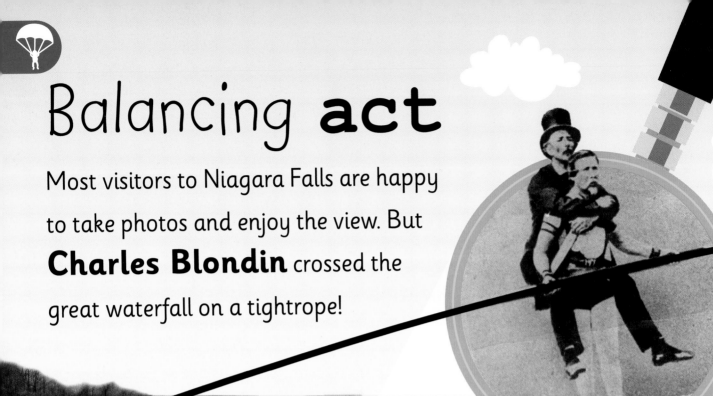

Blindfolded

Carrying someone

The fearless Frenchman became an acrobat when he was just five years old. He was known as "The Boy Wonder."

Walking a tightrope

In 1859, Blondin made history by crossing the dangerous Niagara Falls on the America-Canada border, on a tightrope without safety nets or harnesses. During the stunt, he stopped to have a drink and **take photos** of the crowd!

Blondin's manager (who Blondin once carried across the falls on his back) described Blondin as "more like a fantastic sprite than a human being."

Aerial adventurer

The daredevil had so much fun that he kept coming up with new ways to **wow audiences**. He crossed the falls while blindfolded, carrying people, walking backward, pushing a wheelbarrow, and cooking and eating an omelet!

Walking backward

Pushing a wheelbarrow

Eating at a table

Blondin's tightrope was 160 ft (48 m) above the water—about the height of 10 giraffes!

The word for a tightrope walker is "funambulist."

The Great Blondin

Blondin's act attracted the attention of princes and presidents. Crowds **bet money** on whether he would fall to his death, but in the 300 times he crossed the falls he never did. Blondin died peacefully at 72 nowhere near a wire!

201

The human cannonball

How would you feel about being blasted **out of a cannon**? This high-flying acrobat made history by doing just that as a teenager in 1877.

Aerial adventurer

Born in London in 1863, **Rossa Matilda Richter** knew early on she didn't want to live an "ordinary" life. She became an actress and acrobat, and was soon performing tricks on the trapeze and the tightrope. At 14 years old, she took the stage name **Zazel**.

Explosive gunpowder sounds were played during her act to enhance the performance.

Zazel performed her act for audiences more than 1,000 times.

The big night

Zazel wanted to make history, and decided to become the first person to be fired out of a cannon. Big crowds gathered to watch her, and, after a loud **bang**, Zazel flew 20 ft (6 m) into the air before landing in a safety net.

In reality, there wasn't an explosion—the "cannon" contained a powerful spring.

Highs and lows

Zazel's high-flying act was dangerous, and during one performance she fell and broke her back. Although she recovered, she never performed again. Despite the sad ending, this fearless acrobat is remembered as a **shooting star**.

Pioneering parachutist

This fearless teenager jumped at the opportunity to become the **first woman** to parachute from an airplane.

Jumping for joy

Born in the US in 1893, **Georgia Thompson** was nicknamed **Tiny** because of her size. As a teenager, "Tiny" loved watching traveling shows where daredevils performed stunts. At 15, she asked Charles Broadwick, the manager of a parachuting show, if she could join his company and he agreed.

Tiny became the star of the show, enthralling audiences by leaping from balloons.

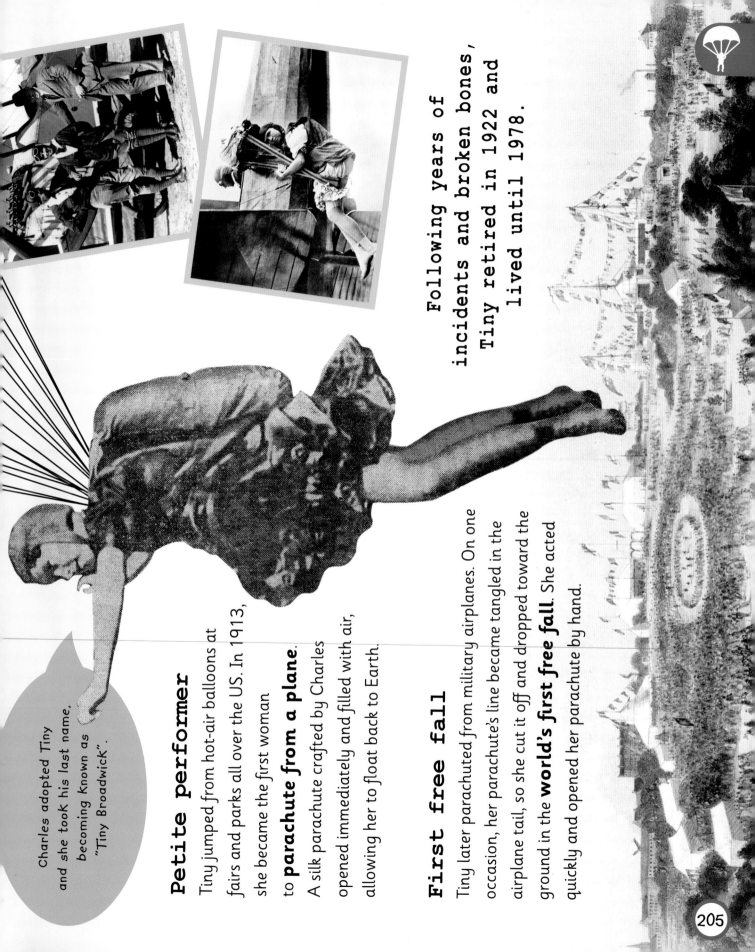

Charles adopted Tiny and she took his last name, becoming known as "Tiny Broadwick".

Petite performer

Tiny jumped from hot-air balloons at fairs and parks all over the US. In 1913, she became the first woman to **parachute from a plane**.

A silk parachute crafted by Charles opened immediately and filled with air, allowing her to float back to Earth.

First free fall

Tiny later parachuted from military airplanes. On one occasion, her parachute's line became tangled in the airplane tail, so she cut it off and dropped toward the ground in the **world's first free fall**. She acted quickly and opened her parachute by hand.

Following years of incidents and broken bones, Tiny retired in 1922 and lived until 1978.

The expert of escape

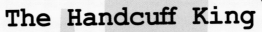

Harry Houdini

This master of illusion stunned audiences around the world by performing sensational stunts and **unbelievable escapes**.

The Handcuff King

Born in Hungary in 1874, Erik Weisz moved to the US when he was four. When he grew up, he became a **magician** and **escape artist**, adopting the stage name **Harry Houdini**. He found early fame by escaping from handcuffs on stage, earning him the nickname "The Handcuff King."

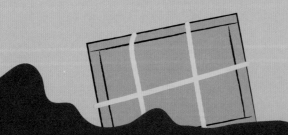

Watch out!

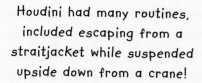

Houdini had many routines, included escaping from a straitjacket while suspended upside down from a crane!

Underwater escape

In 1912, Houdini developed one of his most **famous** escape routines. He was willingly handcuffed, nailed inside a wooden box, and dropped into New York's East River! Just minutes later, he amazed the crowd by surfacing with his arms free of the handcuffs!

In reality, Houdini was out of the handcuffs before his box had been nailed shut!

How will he get out of this?

Magic or trick?

How did Houdini escape the box? The key was a **secret trapdoor** that allowed him to get out and swim to safety. The routine was still **dangerous**—on one occasion, the box landed with the trapdoor in the mud, making his escape more difficult!

Barreling into history

Some people take huge risks to make money. **Annie Edson Taylor** came up with one of the biggest!

The master plan

Annie was born in 1838 into a wealthy American family but, always feared becoming poor. In 1901, she hatched a plan she hoped would make her rich: becoming the first person to survive a trip over **Niagara Falls**—one of the largest waterfalls in the world.

Annie spent many years working as a schoolteacher before attempting her daredevil feat.

The moment of truth

Annie planned to make the **dangerous drop** inside a wooden barrel. On her 63rd birthday, she was lowered from a boat into the water, and the current quickly took her. She plunged down the falls and was successfully rescued with very few injuries.

The barrel was built from sturdy oak and strengthened with iron straps. Annie also put a mattress inside.

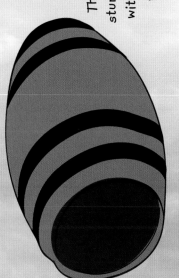

Annie's grave is located in New York, in an area of the cemetery reserved for people who have performed dangerous stunts.

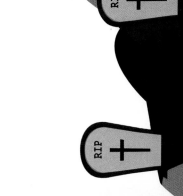

Short-lived success

Despite becoming the first person to survive a fall over Niagara, the **fortune** Annie hoped to earn sadly never came.

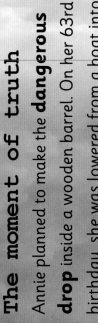

Queen of The Mist

Flying high

This fearless **wing walker** performed bold and daring stunts for a sea of stunned spectators.

Lillian Boyer

Flying start

Born in the US in 1901, **Lillian Boyer** worked as a waitress, but her life took an unexpected turn when a customer asked her to come flying. She loved the excitement of being in the air, and the next time she went flying she climbed outside and walked along the wing of the airplane! It wasn't long before she became a professional wing walker.

"I never had any fear at all."
—Lillian Boyer

Daring acrobatics

From 1921 to 1928, Lillian took to the skies in a plane flown by World War I fighter pilot Billy Brock. Each time, Lillian's daredevil feats became ever more **dangerous**. She hung from the plane by her toes, balanced on her head, and even jumped from airplane to airplane!

Woo-hoo!

The fearless Lillian also loved parachute jumping.

High profile

This rising star soon hit the headlines. Alongside Billy, she started her own circus show and performed daring stunts in more than **350 wing-walking displays** across the US and Canada.

Boyer claimed the audience loved it best when she hung on by her teeth!

Super stuntman

In 1967, motorcycle daredevil **Evel Knievel** raced along a takeoff ramp at Caesar's Palace casino in Las Vegas, US. He was trying to launch himself over two huge fountains. Would he make it?

The jump

Evel had attempted many dangerous motorcycle jumps before, but this was his **biggest**. A large crowd assembled and held their breath as Evel, dressed in his trademark red, white, and blue leather jumpsuit, shot through the air.

Safety snag

Evel cleared the fountains, but as he landed, his back wheel **snagged** on the safety ramp. He flew over his handlebars and tumbled across the ground. He was rushed to the hospital with many broken bones, and was bedridden for a month.

I wasn't going to give up that easily! I recovered, got back on my bike, and performed many more stunts to entertain audiences over the years.

A few years later, Evel Knievel jumped over 13 buses at Wembley Stadium, England!

Evel Knievel

As a boy, Evel Knievel's first motorcycle stunt was jumping over a box of rattlesnakes!

Supersonic superstar

**Boo**

Imagine traveling the length of three football fields in a single second! This American pilot did just that and became the first person to fly faster than the **speed of sound**.

Plucky pilot

The sky was always the limit for **Chuck Yeager**. After joining the United States Air Force in 1941, he became a fighter pilot and took part in 64 missions during World War II. He shot down enemy airplanes and his own plane was shot down over France.

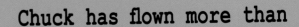Chuck has flown more than

OM!

When Chuck broke the sound barrier, the shock waves from his airplane created an incredibly loud noise known as a "sonic boom."

Speed of sound

After the war, Chuck worked as a test pilot for different airplanes. In October 1947, he flew **faster than the speed of sound**, which is 767 mph (1,234 kph). This flight broke the sound barrier for the first time, ensuring Chuck's name was firmly in the history books. Six years later, he flew at more than double the speed of sound!

"No risk is too great to prevent the necessary job from getting done."
— Chuck Yeager

When Chuck was 89 years old, he repeated his record-breaking flight in the back seat of another airplane!

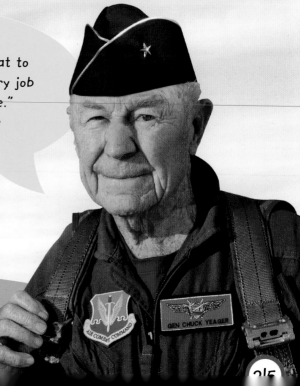

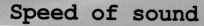

200 different TYPES OF AIRPLANE.

The jump from space

The number of people who have been to space isn't very big, and the number of people who jumped back to Earth? That's **even smaller**. But Felix Baumgartner isn't like most people.

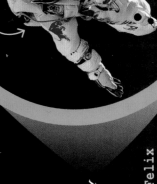

Felix's suit was outfitted with cameras and an oxygen tank.

Special suit

Felix

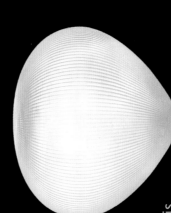

Austrian daredevil Felix Baumgartner was the first person to **skydive** from the edge of space. But before he made his jump, he had to find a way to get there...

Baumgartner and a team of scientists spent years planning every detail. They decided the best way to reach the edge of space was in a special **hot-air balloon**. They also invented a special suit for Felix to wear.

127,852 ft (38,970 m)
Felix's jump height

On October 15, 2012, after years of planning, Felix, in a capsule attached to the biggest hot-air balloon ever made, rose about 24 miles (39 km) in the sky. After final preparations, Felix **jumped**....

As he plummeted to Earth, Felix reached a speed of 833 mph (1,342 kph). After a **nine minute** free fall, he opened his parachute and landed safely.

The height Felix jumped from was four times higher than an airplane flies.

Mount Everest

There's a reason people call me "Fearless Felix."

Millions of people watched a livestream of Felix's daring dive.

Extreme climbing

If you thought climbing a tree was hard, imagine climbing a giant granite rock with no ropes to catch you if you fall. That's what **Alex Honnold** did when he climbed El Capitan, a cliff face in Yosemite National Park, US.

When someone climbs a cliff face with no equipment, it's called a "free solo." The climber must rely on strength and skill alone. It's very dangerous.

Practice makes perfect

American climber Alex Honnold trained hard before his climb. Several times a week, he would spend an hour hanging from his fingertips to make them strong enough to hold onto the smallest cracks in the cliff face. He thoroughly researched his route and did more than 40 **practice climbs** before he felt ready to attempt it without ropes.

The ascent

In 2017, Alex started his climb with nothing but a bag of chalk to keep his hands dry. He had to hold onto cracks with his **fingertips**, squeeze his body through narrow spaces, and tiptoe on ledges thinner than matchboxes.

El Capitan

El Capitan in the US is taller than Burj Khalifa in Dubai, UAE—the tallest building in the world!

Alex's route

Burj Khalifa

Straight to the top

It takes most climbers several days to climb El Capitan with climbing equipment. Alex did it in a single morning with no equipment at all! He is the **first** and **only** person to free solo climb El Capitan.

Alex

Alex was filmed while he scaled El Capitan. The movie, *Free Solo*, went on to win an Oscar!

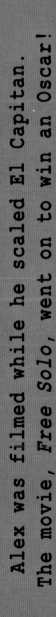

Index

Acknowledgments

The publisher would like to thank the following for their kind permission to reproduce their photographs:

(Key: a-above; b-below/bottom; c-center; f-far; l-left; r-right; t-top)

1 123RF.com: Stasyuk Stanislav (tr). **Dreamstime.com:** Blue Ring Education Pte Ltd (bl); Eddydegroot (b). **2 iStockphoto.com:** proxyminder (tl). **3 Dorling Kindersley:** Roskilde Viking Ships Museum, Denmark (br). **Fotolia:** Dundanim (tr). **5 123RF.com:** Pablo Hidalgo (bc); Alberto Loyo (cb). **Dorling Kindersley:** Mangala Purushottam (tr). **Dreamstime.com:** Fredweiss (cb/Camel). **iStockphoto.com:** serts (br). **6 Dreamstime.com:** Tacettin Ulas / Photofactoryulas (cb). **7 123RF.com:** Triken (bc). **Dreamstime.com:** Azuzl (bc/Mushroom). **8 Alamy Stock Photo:** View Stock (l). **Dorling Kindersley:** Roskilde Viking Ships Museum, Denmark (br). **Dreamstime. com:** Brancaescova (cra). **9 Alamy Stock Photo:** Classic Image (cb, crb); The Picture Art Collection (ca); IanDagnall Computing (cra). **10 Alamy Stock Photo:** Imaginechina Limited (l). **11 Alamy Stock Photo:** The History Collection (br); Imaginechina Limited (cra, bc). **12 Dreamstime.com:** Boris Zerwann (tl). **13 Alamy Stock Photo:** All Canada Photos (tr). **Dorling Kindersley:** Roskilde Viking Ships Museum, Denmark (b). **14-15 Dreamstime.com:** Vvo (Background). **14 Alamy Stock Photo:** Classic Image (cra); Granger Historical Picture Archive (c). **Dreamstime.com:** Veremer (b). **15 Alamy Stock Photo:** Classic Image (cl, ca, c, br). **Getty Images:** Art Media / Print Collector (cra). **16 123RF.com:** Christos Georghiou / Krisdog (t/Background). **Dreamstime.com:** Ahmad Faizal Yahya / Afby71 (crb); Jeneses Imre (tr); Bodik1992 (t); Bbgreg (b). **16-17 123RF.com:** Andreykuzmin (Background). **17 123RF. com:** Attila Mittl / atee83 (bc, cra); Sergey Galushko / galdzer (tr); Christos Georghiou / Krisdog (Background). **Dreamstime.com:** Bodik1992 (bl); Jeneses Imre (c). **18 Alamy Stock Photo:** Peter Horree (cl). **Dorling Kindersley:** Durham University Oriental Museum (br); Science Museum, London (clb). **Dreamstime.com:** Jeneses Imre (cb). **18-19 Dreamstime.com:** Jeneses Imre (Boat). **iStockphoto.com:** CHUYN (cb). **19 123RF.com:** Aaron Amat (cr); Anan Kaewkhammul (cb). **Dorling Kindersley:** Blackpool Zoo, Lancashire, UK (crb). **Dreamstime.com:** Yinan Zhang (tr). **Getty Images:** DE Agostini Picture Library (ca). **20 Alamy Stock Photo:** Classic Image (tc). **21 Alamy Stock Photo:** IanDagnall Computing (tr); The Picture Art Collection (b). **Dreamstime.com:** Carla Zagni (tl). **22-23 123RF.com:** Eleonora Konnova (Background). **22 Alamy Stock Photo:** The Granger Collection (cra); Lanmas (crb). **Dreamstime.com:** Nevinates (cb). **23 Alamy Stock Photo:** Lanmas (t, c). **Dreamstime.com:** Javarman (b). **24 Alamy Stock Photo:** Granger Historical Picture Archive (cl). **24-25 Dreamstime.com:** Mishoo (t). **25 Alamy Stock Photo:** Granger Historical Picture Archive (crb). **iStockphoto.com:** duncan1890 (cl, cr). **26 Alamy Stock Photo:** View Stock (l/Mt. Wuyi). **Dreamstime.com:** Frenta (b); Lynn Watson / Luckydog1 (l). **26-27 Dreamstime.com:** Xianghong Wu / Wxh6763 (t). **27 Alamy Stock Photo:** Tim Graham (crb). **Dreamstime.com:** Sabelskaya (cr). **28-29 Alamy Stock Photo:** North Wind Picture Archives. **Dreamstime.com:** Mishoo (t). **29 Alamy Stock Photo:** GL Archive (c). **Dreamstime.com:** Vasyl Helevachuk (crb). **30-31 Dorling Kindersley:** Mangala Purushottam (t). **30 Alamy Stock Photo:** Agefotostock (ca); Chronicle (bl). **Getty Images:** Hulton Archive (cr). **31 Alamy Stock Photo:** Agefotostock (ca). **32 123RF.com:** Stanislav Odiagailo (cl). **Alamy Stock Photo:** Granger Historical Picture Archive (br); Pictorial Press Ltd (cla); The Natural History Museum (c/Beetles). **Dreamstime.com:** Coffeechocolates (c); Evgeniya Kramar (r). **32-33 123RF.com:** lightwise. **Dreamstime.com:** Daboost (Notebook); Sergiy Bykhunenko / Sbworld4 (wood texture). **33 123RF.com:** Eduardo Rivero / edurivero (tr); eleter (tl). **Alamy Stock Photo:** The Natural History Museum (clb). **Dreamstime.

com:** Jakkapan Jabjainai (t/Paper); Channarong Pherngjanda (fcr); Odua (cr). **iStockphoto.com:** proxyminder (b). **34-35 Dreamstime.com:** Jeneses Imre (t, b). **34 123RF.com:** David Benes (crb); Storyimage (bl). **Dreamstime.com:** Hugoht (Flag). **35 123RF.com:** Storyimage (br). **Alamy Stock Photo:** Interfoto (br/game); Lebrecht Music & Arts (ca). **36-37 123RF.com:** Nataliia Anisimova (b/Background). **36 Alamy Stock Photo:** Chronicle (c); Hirarchivum Press (l). **37 Depositphotos Inc:** interactimages (cra). **38-39 Dreamstime.com:** Andreykuzmin (Background). **38 Alamy Stock Photo:** Science History Images (br). **Dreamstime.com:** Aleksandar Mirkovic (tr, cra). **39 123RF.com:** Adrian Bidea (ca, cla). **Alamy Stock Photo:** Pictures Now (cb). **Dreamstime.com:** Aleksandar Mirkovic (ca/Tree). **41 123RF.com:** Tracy Fox / rfoxfoto (cr). **Alamy Stock Photo:** IanDagnall Computing (cl). **42-43 Dreamstime.com:** Znm (c). **42 Alamy Stock Photo:** Paul Brown (bl). **Dreamstime. com:** Brancaescova (c). **43 Dreamstime.com:** Frank Bach (tr); Znm (bc). **44-45 123RF.com:** Sergey Nivens (t). **Dreamstime.com:** Rozum (b/Background). **44 Alamy Stock Photo:** Granger Historical Picture Archive (cr); Niday Picture Library (l); Science History Images (tc). **45 Alamy Stock Photo:** Archive Pics (clb); Niday Picture Library (tl); The History Collection (cra). **46 Dreamstime.com:** B1e2n3i4 (c). **46-47 Alamy Stock Photo:** TheImage (Background). **47 Alamy Stock Photo:** Classic Image (t, ca); World History Archive (bc). **48 Alamy Stock Photo:** Colport (cra). **Getty Images:** Frank Krahmer / Photographer's Choice RF (cl); Frank Hurley / Royal Geographical Society (cra). **49 123RF.com:** Eleonora Konnova (tr). **Alamy Stock Photo:** Incamerastock (bl). **50 Getty Images:** Hulton Archive (c). **iStockphoto.com:** serts (l). **50-51 123RF.com:** Aleksandr Frolov (b/Background). **iStockphoto.com:** Kerrick (t/Background). **51 Dorling Kindersley:** Durham University Oriental Museum (c). **Dreamstime.com:** Jaroslav Moravcik (cr). **Getty Images:** Mansell / Mansell / The LIFE Picture Collection (clb); Hulton-Deutsch Collection / Corbis (cla). **52 Alamy Stock Photo:** Keystone Press (cl). **52-53 Dreamstime.com:** Daniel Prudek (Background). **53 123RF.com:** Oleg Breslavtsev (c). **Alamy Stock Photo:** Tim Cuff (bl, fbr). **Getty Images:** Bettmann (crb). **54 Alamy Stock Photo:** Sputnik (cb). **Getty Images:** Bettmann (cl). **56 Alamy Stock Photo:** NASA Archive (bl). **57 Alamy Stock Photo:** NASA Archive (br); Science History Images (t); The Print Collector (cla, cra). **Dorling Kindersley:** NASA (fcra). **58-59 Alamy Stock Photo:** Oleksiy Maksymenko Photography. **58 Getty Images:** Ingo Jezierski / Photodisc (bc). **59 Alamy Stock Photo:** incamerastock (br). **Getty Images:** STR / AFP (cra). **60-61 123RF.com:** gkuna (b/Background); Tommaso Lizzul (b). **Getty Images:** Rick Smolan / Contour. **61 Dreamstime.com:** Bennymarty (cr); Fredweiss (cl). **62 Alamy Stock Photo:** imageBROKER (tl); yvo (cl). **62-63 Dreamstime.com:** Albund (t). **63 Dreamstime. com:** Dmitry Pichugin / Dmitryp (ca); Ecelop (crb). **64 Dreamstime.com:** Yevgeniy Ill'yin (cl). **Getty Images:** Imeh Akpanudosen (bl). **64-65 Dreamstime.com:** Daniela Spyropoulou / Dana. **65 Alamy Stock Photo:** Photo 12 (tc). **Dreamstime.com:** Sabri Deniz Kizil / Bogalo. **66 123RF.com:** tawhy (crb/Dynamite). **Alamy Stock Photo:** Granger Historical Picture Archive (bl); Heritage Image Partnership Ltd (crb). **Dreamstime.com:** Lineartestpilot (crb/Scientist illustration). **67 Alamy Stock Photo:** Chronicle (c). **Dreamstime.com:** Torian Dixon / Mrincredible (cra). **68 Alamy Stock Photo:** Classic Image (cr). **68-69 123RF.com:** Oxana Lebedeva (Background). **69 Alamy Stock Photo:** (cb). **Dreamstime.com:** Dauker (c). **70 Alamy Stock Photo:** Vicky Barlow (cr); Lebrecht Music & Arts (l). **71 Alamy Stock Photo:** Peter Horree (cr); Lanmas (l). **72 Alamy Stock Photo:** Pictorial Press Ltd (cla). **72-73 Alamy Stock Photo:** Chronicle (b). **73 123RF.com:** Camilo Maranchᣳn garcÃa (tl). **Alamy Stock Photo:** ART Collection (cb). **Dreamstime.com:** Destina156 (tc/Pluto); Forplayday (tc). **74 Alamy Stock Photo:** Science History Images (br). **Getty Images:** Hulton Archive (cr). **74-75 123RF.com:** solarseven (b). **75 Alamy Stock Photo:** Darling Archive (cla);

223

123RF.com: Stasyuk Stanislav (cra). **Alamy Stock Photo:** The Picture Art Collection (l). **iStockphoto.com:** koya79 (cla). **153 123RF.com:** Triken (cla). **Alamy Stock Photo:** Agefotostock (ca/Piano); Lakeview Images (ca); Hemis (br). **154 Alamy Stock Photo:** imageBROKER (bc). **Getty Images:** BJI / Blue Jean Images (r/Girl). **iStockphoto.com:** Riorita (r). **155 123RF.com:** Patrick Guenette (fcla, ca, cra). **Alamy Stock Photo:** Hemis (br); imageBROKER (tc). **Dreamstime.com:** Jolanta Dabrowska (c). **156 123RF.com:** hancess (l). **156-157 123RF.com:** Eleonora Konnova (ca/Paper). **157 Alamy Stock Photo:** Xuguang Wang (br). **Dreamstime.com:** Pierre Aden (bl). **158-159 iStockphoto.com:** Explora_2005. **158 Alamy Stock Photo:** Ihsan Gercelman (bl). **159 Alamy Stock Photo:** Peter Horree (br). **160 Alamy Stock Photo:** Ancient Art and Architecture (bl). **160-161 Dreamstime.com:** Eddydegroot (b). **162 Alamy Stock Photo:** Pictorial Press Ltd (cb). **Dreamstime.com:** Blue Ring Education Pte Ltd (l/Jungle). **162-163 Dreamstime.com:** Jarnogz (c). **163 Alamy Stock Photo:** Rubens Alarcon (cb). **Getty Images:** Prisma / Universal Images Group (cra). **164 Alamy Stock Photo:** Michele Falzone (bl). **Getty Images:** Livio ANTICOLI / Gamma-Rapho. **165 Alamy Stock Photo:** IanDagnall Computing (crb). **166 123RF.com:** Lakhesis (tr). **Alamy Stock Photo:** Lakeview Images (br). **Dreamstime.com:** Elisanth (tr/Moon). **167 Alamy Stock Photo:** Agefotostock (b); GL Archive (cra). **168-169 123RF.com:** Derek Simpson (t). **Dreamstime.com:** Julia Shevchenko / Laracraft. **168 123RF.com:** Triken (crb). **Alamy Stock Photo:** The Print Collector (tr). **Dreamstime.com:** Azuzl (br). **iStockphoto.com:** duncan1890 (bl). **169 123RF.com:** Olga Popova (cb); Triken (tc). **Alamy Stock Photo:** Keith Corrigan (tc/Anne Anderson); INTERFOTO (tl); North Wind Picture Archives (cl); Historical image collection by Bildagentur-online (c). **Dreamstime.com:** Regina555 (ca). **iStockphoto.com:** ZU_09 (br). **170 Alamy Stock Photo:** GL Archive (tl). **170-171 Dreamstime.com:** Irochka (cb). **172 123RF.com:** Antonio Guillem (bl); Lev Kropotov (tr). **Alamy Stock Photo:** Science History Images (r). **iStockphoto.com:** pterwort (clb). **172-173 iStockphoto.com:** CynthiaAnnF (b). **173 123RF.com:** Singkam Chanteb (cr). **Getty Images:** PhotoQuest (clb). **iStockphoto.com:** zygotehasnobrain (br). **174 Getty Images:** Oxford Science Archive / Print Collector (clb, cl). **174-175 iStockphoto.com:** Kerrick (t). **175 Alamy Stock Photo:** The Picture Art Collection (bl). **Dreamstime.com:** Leungphotography (crb); Andrey Simonenko. **iStockphoto.com:** koya79 (cl). **176 Alamy Stock Photo:** Everett Collection Historical (cl); NPS Photo (cr). **176-177 iStockphoto.com:** Kerrick (c). **177 Alamy Stock Photo:** Brian Lawrence (cra); Universal Art Archive (cb). **iStockphoto.com:** Radionphoto (cb). **178 Alamy Stock Photo:** Hi-Story (br). **iStockphoto.com:** duncan1890 (tr). **178-179 123RF.com:** Stasyuk Stanislav (tc). **179 Dreamstime.com:** (cl); Vladimir Yudin (c). **Getty Images:** Bettmann (bc). **180 Alamy Stock Photo:** Granger Historical Picture Archive (cb). **181 Alamy Stock Photo:** Granger Historical Picture Archive (tl); Pictorial Press Ltd. **182 123RF.com:** Roystudio (b). **Alamy Stock Photo:** History and Art Collection (cb). **Getty Images:** Apic (br). **iStockphoto.com:** TomasSereda (cl). **182-183 Dreamstime.com:** Marcorubino. **183 Dreamstime.com:** (t); Kyolshin (bl). **184 123RF.com:** Ten Theeralerttham / rawangtak (bl). **Dorling Kindersley:** Jerry Young (b). **184-185 Dreamstime.com:** Sabri Deniz Kizil / Bogalo (b/Animals). **185 123RF.com:** Ten Theeralerttham / rawangtak (br). **Alamy Stock Photo:** Wilf Doyle (cr/Ship); Granger Historical Picture Archive (c). **Getty Images:** Benjamin Auger / Paris Match (br/Jacques-Yves Cousteau). **186 Dreamstime.com:** Boris Zerwann (l). **Getty Images:** Hulton Archive (tr). **iStockphoto.com:** Sylwia (bl). **186-187 Dreamstime.com:** Luminis. **187 Alamy Stock Photo:** Homer Sykes (br). **Dreamstime.com:** Jktu21 (tr). **iStockphoto.com:** tiler84 (cr). **188 Dorling Kindersley:** Museum of Design in Plastics, Bournemouth Arts University, UK (crb). **Dreamstime.com:** Polinaraulina. **189 iStockphoto.com:** traveler1116 (cra). **190-191 Alamy Stock Photo:** Imaginechina

Limited (b). **192-193 123RF.com:** kritchanut (b); olegdudko. **192 Dreamstime.com:** Joachim Eckel (cl). **Getty Images:** Brenton Geach / Gallo Images (cra); Jeff Christensen / Liaison (cr). **193 Alamy Stock Photo:** Joerg Boethling (ca). **Getty Images:** Jamie McCarthy / Getty Images for Bill & Melinda Gates Foundation (br). **194 123RF.com:** gioiak2 (fcl). **Alamy Stock Photo:** Chronicle (cla); IanDagnall Computing (cl); Science History Images (bl); Everett Collection Inc. **194-195 Alamy Stock Photo:** Science History Images (ca). **196 Alamy Stock Photo:** incamerastock (bl). **Getty Images:** Historica Graphica Collection / Heritage Images (tl). **196-197 123RF.com:** Vassiliy Prikhodko. **Alamy Stock Photo:** Shawshots (b). **Getty Images:** Historica Graphica Collection / Heritage Images (tc). **197 Dreamstime.com:** Marius Droppert / Mariusdroppert (clb). **Getty Images:** DeAgostini (cra); Sepia Times / Universal Images Group (l). **198 Alamy Stock Photo:** Chronicle (c). **iStockphoto.com:** Kerrick (bl/Background). **198-199 123RF.com:** Aivolie (ca). **Alamy Stock Photo:** Frances Roberts (b). **199 iStockphoto.com:** Nosyrevy (tr). **200-201 Dreamstime.com:** Elovkoff (Background). **200 Getty Images:** Hulton Archive (cra); Hulton-Deutsch Collection / Corbis (clb). **202-203 Alamy Stock Photo:** Science History Images. **Dreamstime.com:** Tortoon (Background). **204 123RF.com:** Derek Simpson (Background). **Alamy Stock Photo:** Chronicle (c). **Getty Images:** Bettmann (bc). **205 Alamy Stock Photo:** Collection 68 (c); PF-(sdasm4) (tl); Granger Historical Picture Archive (tc). **Getty Images:** SSPL (r). **206 123RF.com:** gioiak2 (cl/Handcuffs). **Alamy Stock Photo:** IanDagnall Computing (cl). **Getty Images:** Peter Keegan / Keystone (tr). **207 Getty Images:** FPG (b). **208 Alamy Stock Photo:** Science History Images (bc, cb). **208-209 Alamy Stock Photo:** Wayne Hutchinson (Background). **209 Alamy Stock Photo:** Science History Images (br). **210-211 Getty Images:** Minnesota Historical Society / Corbis (c). **210 Alamy Stock Photo:** Niday Picture Library (cl). **211 Dreamstime.com:** Lightzoom (br). **Getty Images:** Minnesota Historical Society / Corbis (cla). **212-213 Getty Images:** Bettmann. **213 Dreamstime.com:** Isselee (br). **Getty Images:** Ralph Crane / The LIFE Picture Collection (b); Kypros (cra). **214 Alamy Stock Photo:** Aviation History Collection (l). **214-215 123RF.com:** Derek Simpson (Sky background). **215 Alamy Stock Photo:** PF-(aircraft) (cl); US Air Force Photo (br). **216 Avalon:** Luke Aikins (tr). Rex by Shutterstock: Keystone / Zuma (bl). **217 Alamy Stock Photo:** EDB Image Archive (tr). **Dreamstime.com:** Dmitry Pichugin / Dmitryp; Gv1961 (cl); Irochka (cra). **218-219 123RF.com:** Vassiliy Prikhodko (Background). **Alamy Stock Photo:** TCD / Prod.DB (b). **219 Alamy Stock Photo:** Cavan (cb); George Ward (cla). **220 iStockphoto.com:** Passakorn_14 (cb). **221 123RF.com:** Triken (clb). **Dreamstime.com:** Azuzl (bl). **223 Alamy Stock Photo:** World History Archive (bc). **Dreamstime.com:** Rozum (bl). **Getty Images:** Frank Krahmer / Photographer's Choice RF (crb). **224 Dreamstime.com:** Pierre Aden (b)

Cover images: *Front:* **123RF.com:** Pablo Hidalgo br; **Dorling Kindersley:** Roskilde Viking Ships Museum, Denmark bl; **Fotolia:** Dundanim tr; *Back:* **Dorling Kindersley:** Mangala Purushottam tr; **iStockphoto.com:** proxyminder cl

All other images © Dorling Kindersley
For further information see: www.dkimages.com

DK would like to thank:

Kitty Glavin for additional illustrations. Marie Lorimer for indexing. Sophie Parkes for proofreading. Philip Parker for fact checking. Martin Copeland and Lynne Murray for picture library assistance. Emma Shepherd and Anna Wilson for font assistance.